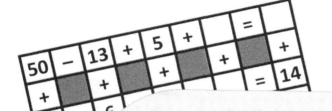

Table of Contents

Sections: Page:

(Answer Key in Back)

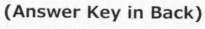

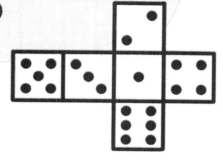

Want something more basic?

Book 1 *focuses on easier patterns and puzzles.*

Mirror Images

A mirror image is like a reflection in a mirror. When you look in a mirror, the same image is reflected but backward. A mirror image in mathematics is the same way. It's the same as the original image but reversed.

Notice that the image of the duck is reversed as well as the letters in the word DUCK. A mirror image reverses every aspect of the image. Try holding something with letters printed on it in front of a mirror at your home.

Line of Reflection

A **line of reflection** is the line over which an image is reflected. A line of reflection does not have to be drawn, but often is to show people where the line of reflection is located. In this book a line of reflection will be represented by a dotted line.

Line of Reflection

Example: *If the image to the left is reflected over the dotted line, what will its mirror image look like?*
Shade option A, B, or C to indicate your answer.

If the image to the left is reflected over the dotted line, what will its mirror image look like?
Shade option A, B, or C to indicate your answer.

Day 2
Mirror Images

Name: _____

If the image to the left is reflected over the dotted line, what will its mirror image look like? Shade option A, B, or C to indicate your answer.

1)   Ⓐ 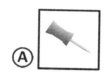 Ⓑ 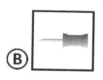 Ⓒ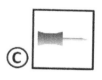

2)   Ⓐ 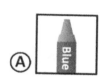 Ⓑ Ⓒ

3)   Ⓐ  Ⓑ Ⓒ

4)  Ⓐ 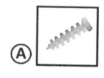 Ⓑ Ⓒ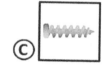

5)   Ⓐ 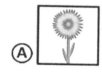 Ⓑ Ⓒ

6)   Ⓐ 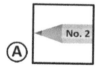 Ⓑ Ⓒ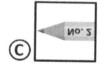

7) Ⓐ  Ⓑ Ⓒ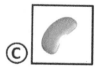

8) Ⓐ  Ⓑ Ⓒ

9) Ⓐ 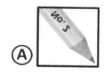 Ⓑ 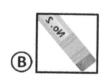 Ⓒ

10) 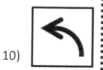 Ⓐ  Ⓑ  Ⓒ

Day 3
Mirror Images

Puzzle

Name: _____

Score:

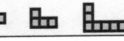

If the image to the left is reflected over the dotted line, what will its mirror image look like?
Shade option A, B, or C to indicate your answer.

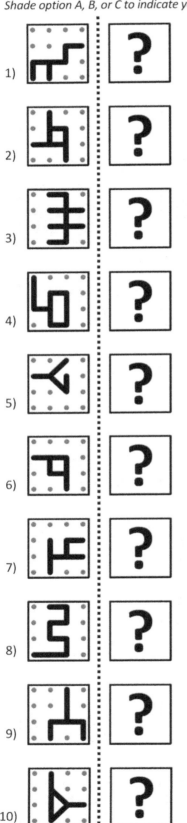

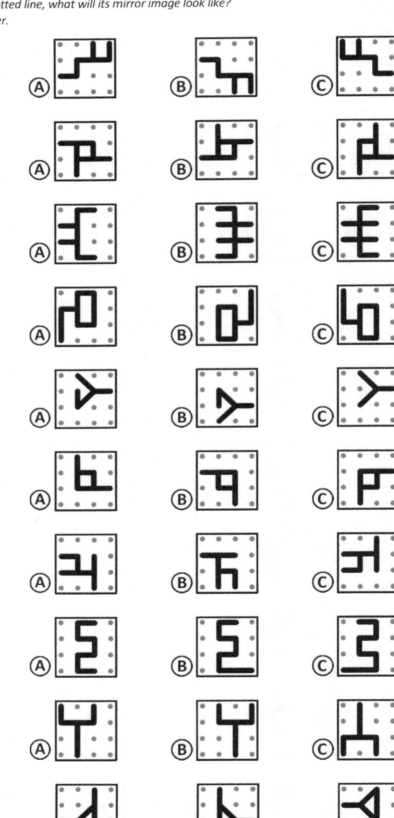

Day 4
Mirror Images

Name: _____

If the image to the left is reflected over the dotted line, what will its mirror image look like? Shade option A, B, or C to indicate your answer.

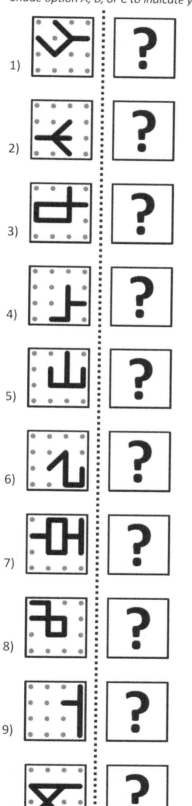

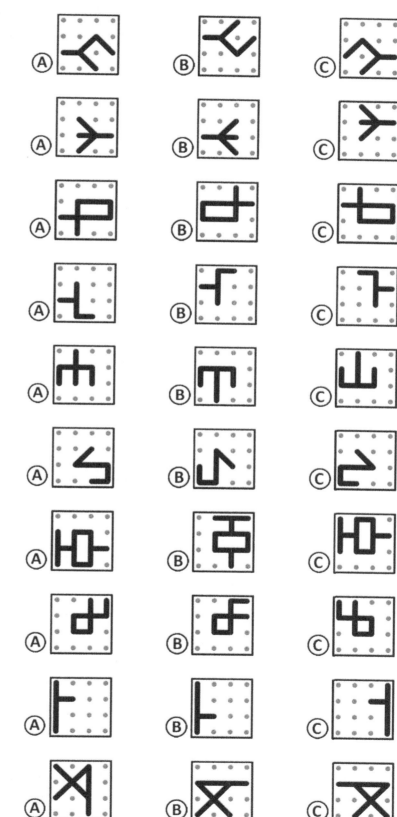

Day 5
Mirror Images

Puzzle

Name: _____

Score:

	22	
9	13	
5	4	9

You Draw the Mirror Image

In the previous pages, the mirror images were drawn for you. Now, you'll be shown an image, and you will need to draw what that image will look like once it is reflected.

Helpful Tips:
1. Imagine what the reflection will look like before you begin to draw.
2. Use a pencil to draw so you can erase mistakes.
3. Use the dots in the image as guides while drawing the necessary lines.
3. Draw your shapes lightly. Darken the shapes after they look the way you want.

Draw how each shape will look after it is reflected over the dotted line.

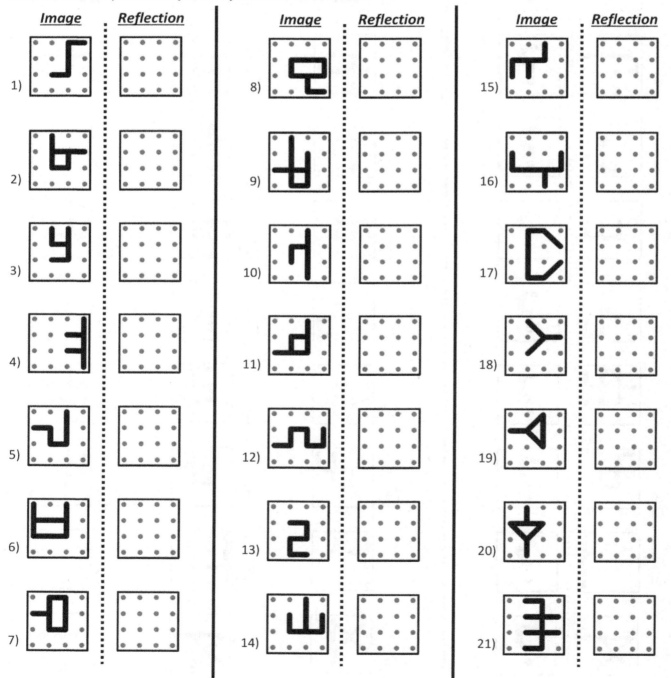

Day 6
Mirror Images

Name: _____

Score:

Draw how each shape will look after it is reflected over the dotted line.

	Image	Reflection		Image	Reflection		Image	Reflection
1)			10)			19)		
2)			11)			20)		
3)			12)			21)		
4)			13)			22)		
5)			14)			23)		
6)			15)			24)		
7)			16)			25)		
8)			17)			26)		
9)			18)			27)		

© Libro Studio LLC 2024

Reflecting Images in Other Directions

So far, an image has been reflected to the right over a line of reflection, but the line of reflection can be located anywhere. A line of reflection could be above, below, or on the left side of the image. Lines of reflection can be positioned diagonally and may even pass over an image too.

The position of the line of reflection influences how the reflection will look. In the problems below, pay attention to where each line of reflection is located (the dotted line). Imagine what the reflection of the image will look like before searching for the correct answer.

If the image is reflected over the dotted line, what will its mirror image look like?
Shade option A, B, or C to indicate your answer.

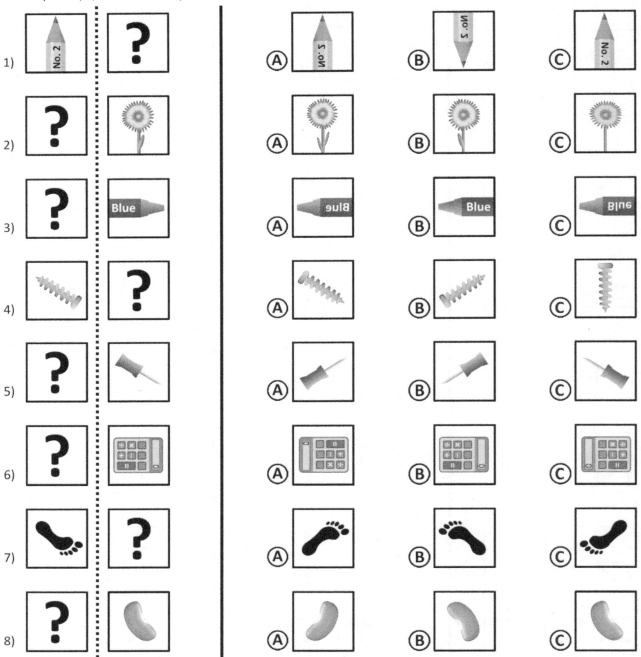

Name: _____

Score:

If the image is reflected over the dotted line, what will its mirror image look like?
Shade option A, B, or C to indicate your answer.

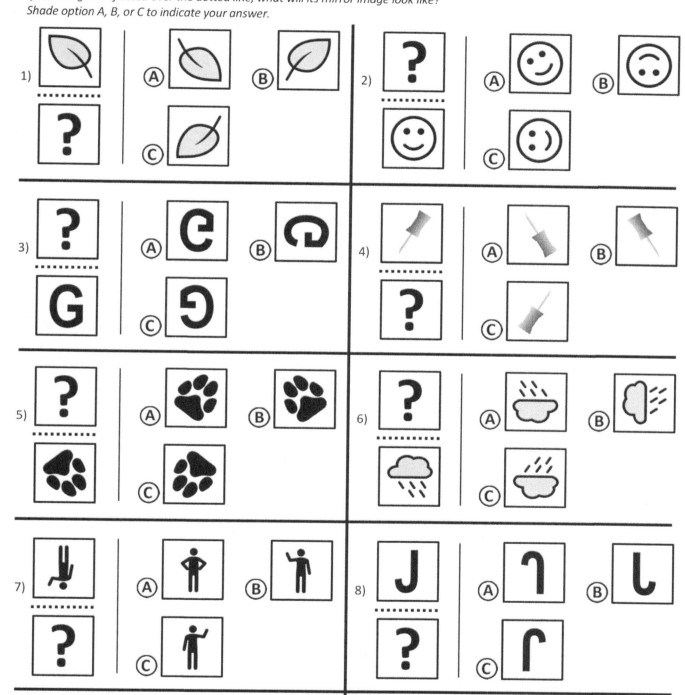

Puzzle
Name: _____
Score:

If the image to the left is reflected over the dotted line, what will its mirror image look like?
Shade option A, B, or C to indicate your answer.

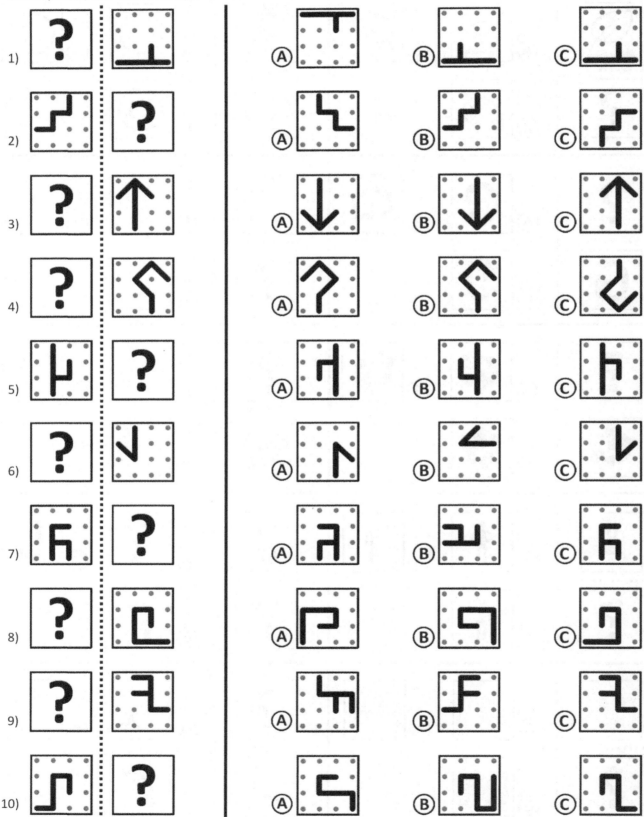

Name: _____

Score:

If the image is reflected over the dotted line, what will its mirror image look like?
Shade option A, B, or C to indicate your answer.

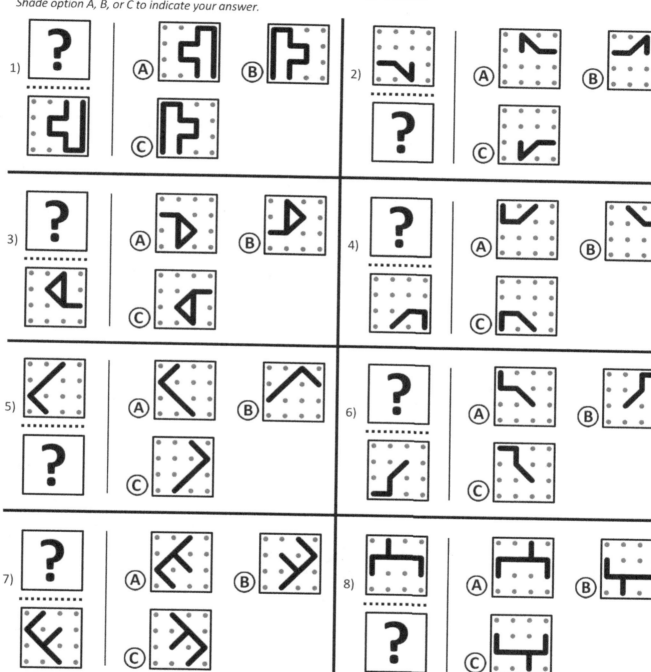

Day 11
Mirror Images

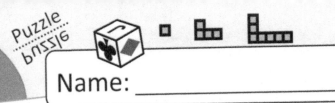

Draw how each shape will look after it is reflected over the dotted line.

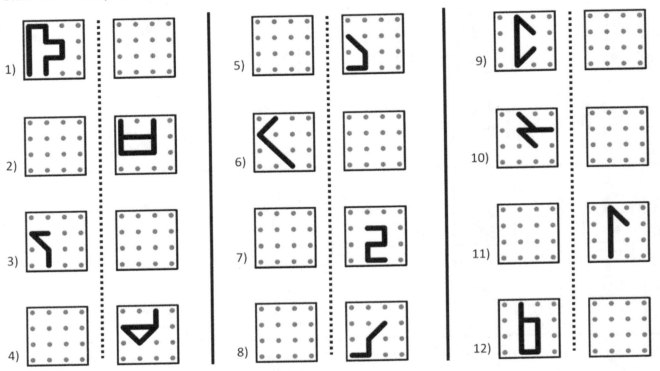

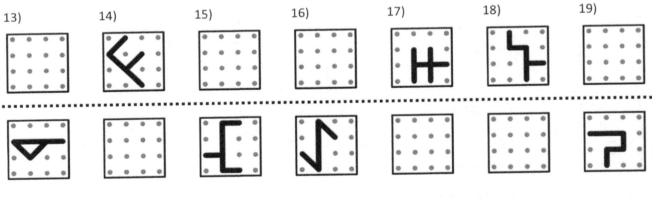

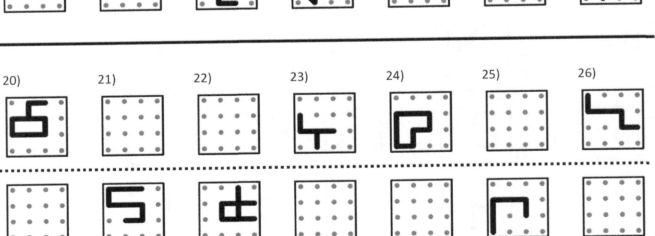

Day 12
Mirror Images

Name: _____

Score:

Draw how each shape will look after it is reflected over the dotted line.

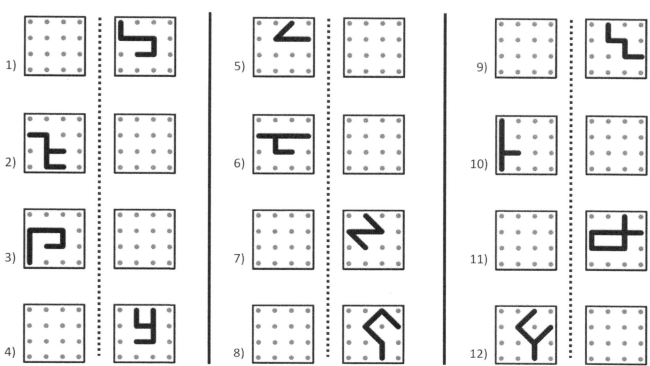

1)
2)
3)
4)
5)
6)
7)
8)
9)
10)
11)
12)

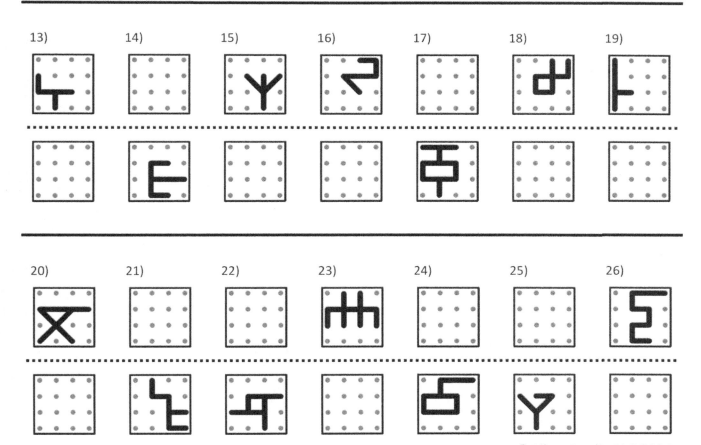

13) 14) 15) 16) 17) 18) 19)

20) 21) 22) 23) 24) 25) 26)

Reflections

Something has **symmetry** when it can be divided into two identical halves that are mirror images of each other. When something has symmetry, it can be described as **symmetrical**. The tree to the left is symmetrical. This tree can be divided into two identical halves.

When something does not have symmetry, it's **asymmetrical**. The tree to the right is asymmetrical. It can't be divided into two identical halves.

Lines of Symmetry

See the dotted line running through the symmetrical tree? That dotted line represents the **line of symmetry**. If the tree were to be folded along this line, the two halves of the tree would match perfectly.

In this example, the line of symmetry is drawn with the dotted line, but the line of symmetry would still exist even if it was not drawn. Drawing the line of symmetry merely helps people realize that the shape is symmetrical and to show them where the line of symmetry is.

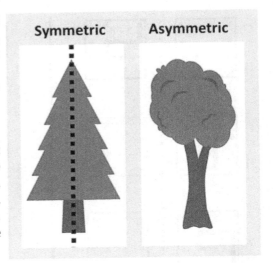

Finding Lines of Symmetry

To find a line of symmetry, you first need to ask yourself if something is symmetrical or not. If it is symmetrical, it can be divided into two identical halves that are mirror images of each other. The line that would divide it in half is the location of the line of symmetry.

If something is not symmetrical, it will not have a line of symmetry.

Some of the shapes below are symmetrical and some are not. The symmetrical shapes on this page will have one line of symmetry. Asymmetrical shapes will not have a line of symmetry.

If the shape is symmetrical, **draw a line** *to indicate where the line of symmetry is. If the shape is asymmetrical,* **do nothing** *to the shape. Leave the asymmetrical shapes alone.*

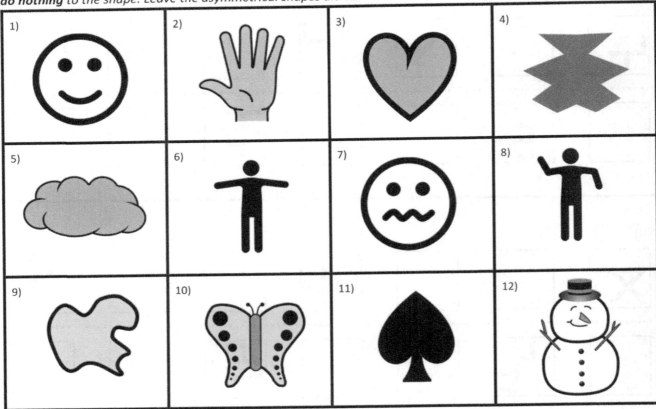

Day 14
Symmetry

Horizontal and Diagonal Lines of Symmetry

In the previous day's practice problems, the lines of symmetry were all **vertical** lines of symmetry. But lines of symmetry can travel in any direction. There can be **horizontal** lines of symmetry or **diagonal** lines of symmetry too.

Pay close attention to the shapes and how they can be divided into equal parts that are mirror images.

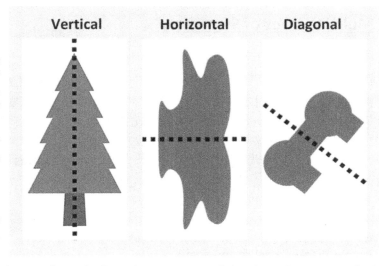

Vertical   Horizontal   Diagonal

Some of the shapes below are symmetrical and some are not. The symmetrical shapes on this page will have one line of symmetry.

*If the shape is symmetrical, **draw a line** to indicate where the line of symmetry is. If the shape is asymmetrical, **do nothing** to the shape. Leave the asymmetrical shapes alone.*

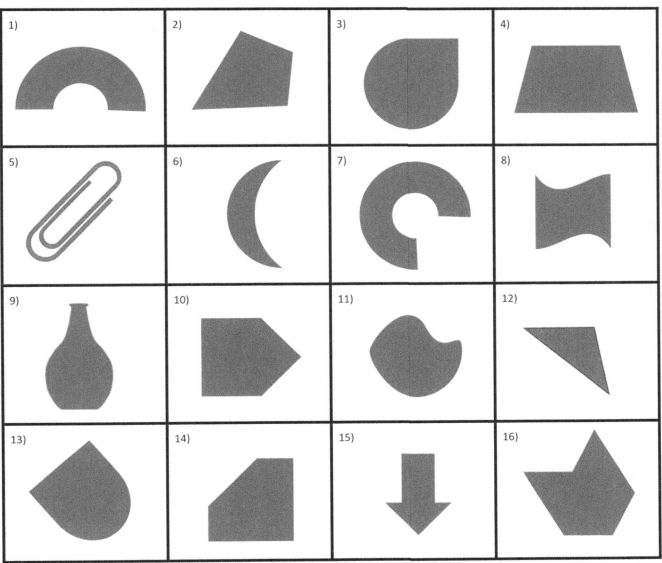

Puzzle

Name: _____

Score:

Multiple Lines of Symmetry

So far, the images have only had one line of symmetry. But images are able to have two, three, or more lines of symmetry too.

Finding All the Lines

Finding all the lines of symmetry can be tricky. There's no easy way to be certain that you've found all the lines of symmetry. Look at each image carefully.

Imagine all the different ways that the image can be divided into equal halves. Don't feel discouraged if you miss some of the lines of symmetry on this page. Finding lines of symmetry takes practice and time.

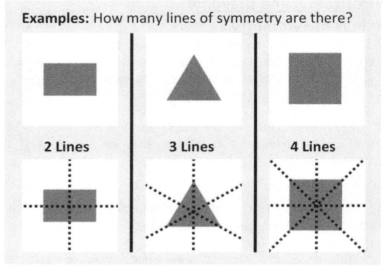

Examples: How many lines of symmetry are there?

2 Lines   3 Lines   4 Lines

All of the shapes below are symmetrical and will have <u>one or more lines of symmetry</u>. Find all their lines of symmetry. **Draw lines** *to indicate where each line of symmetry is located and <u>write how many lines of symmetry the shape has</u>.*

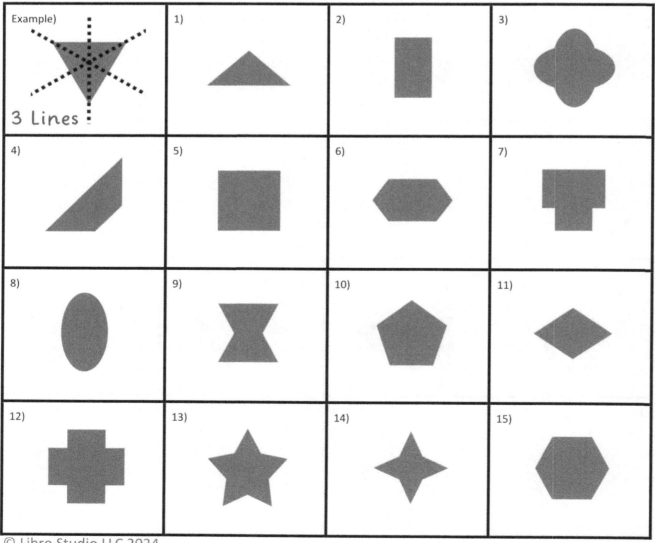

Name: _____

Score:

The Symmetry Letters

Many letters are symmetrical. Depending how the letters are drawn, some letters may have one or more lines of symmetry. Other letters are asymmetrical. They do not have any lines of symmetry.

Some of the letters below are symmetrical and some are not. The symmetrical shapes on this page may have one or more lines of symmetry. Find all their lines of symmetry. **Draw lines** *to indicate where each line of symmetry is located, and* **write how many lines of symmetry the letter has**. *If the letter is asymmetrical,* **do nothing** *to the letter. Leave the asymmetrical shapes alone.*

1) A	2) C	3) D	4) E
5) F	6) G	7) H	8) I
9) J	10) K	11) M	12) N
13) O	14) P	15) T	16) U
17) V	18) W	19) X	20) Y

Puzzle

Name: _____

Score:

Drawing Reflections on Grids

Reflections are often performed on grids. The grid lines can help when measuring and drawing the reflections.

Pay attention to the location of the lines of reflection. Draw the reflection of the shaded squares on the side of the grid that is blank. Once the reflection is drawn, the image on the grid will be symmetrical.

Check your drawing by comparing the two sides of the grid. *Are the two sides mirror images of each other? Is the grid now symmetrical?*

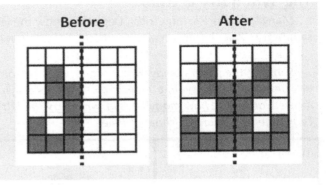

Before   **After**

Draw the reflection by shading the appropriate squares on each grid.

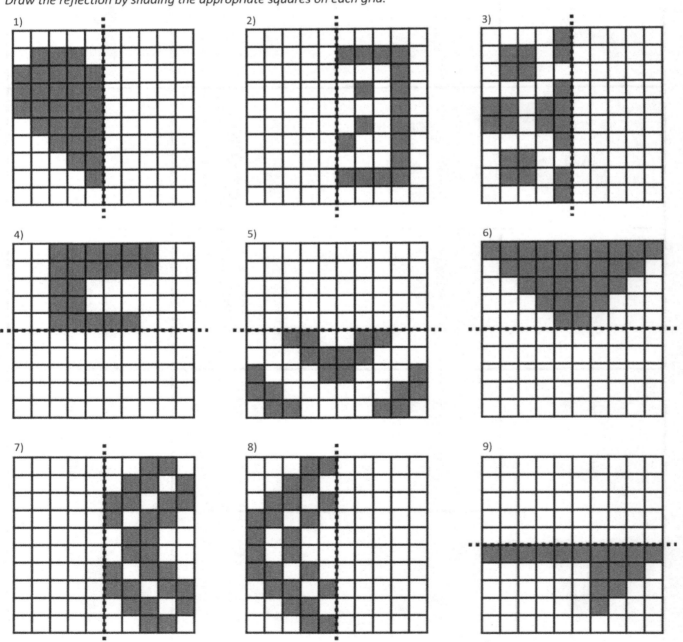

1)

2)

3)

4)

5)

6)

7)

8)

9)

Day 18
Drawing Reflections

Name: _____

Score:

Draw the reflection by shading the appropriate squares on each grid.

1)

2)

3)

4)

5)

6)

7)

8)

9)

10)

11)

12)

Draw the reflection by shading the appropriate squares on each grid.

1)

2)

3)

4)

5)

6)

7)

8)

9)

10)

11)

12)

Day 20
Drawing Reflections

Name: _____

Score:

Design your own symmetrical image. Pay attention to where the line of reflection is.

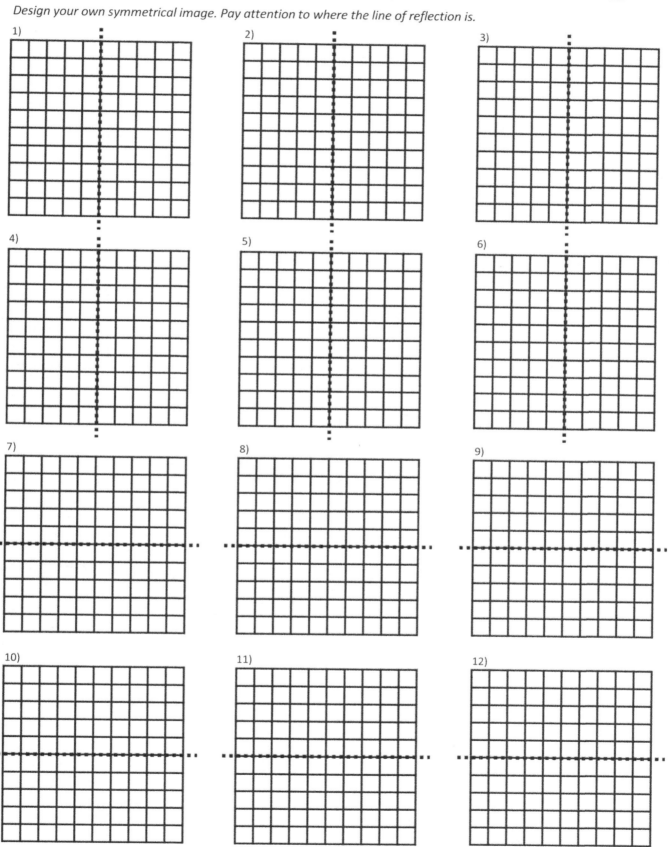

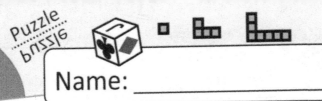

Drawing Reflections without a Grid

Grids are helpful, but not needed to draw a reflection. Do your best to draw what each image will look like when reflected over the line of reflection.

Your drawings do not need to be exact. The main goal is for you to draw the reflection so that it is relatively proportional and reversed compared to the original image.

Try to imagine what each reflection will look like before you begin drawing and use a pencil in case you need to erase parts of your drawing and try again.

Before	After
DAY	DAY
	DAY (reflected)

Draw what each image will look like when reflected over the line of reflection.

1) TOP

2) NOON

3) WOW

4) POOL

5) EAT

6) FUN

7) SAFE

8) MUD

9)

10)

11)

12)

13)

14)

15)

16)

Name: _____

Score:

Draw what each image will look like when reflected over the line of reflection.

1)
TEA ┊

2)
┊ WHY

3)
┊ CAT

4)
┊ YES

5)
FILL ┊

6)
MOM ┊

7)
123 ┊

8)
┊ DOG

9)
BOX ┊

10)

11)

12)

13)

14)

15)

16)

17)

18)

Day 23
Drawing Reflections

Puzzle

Name: _____

Score:

Draw what each image will look like when reflected over the line of reflection.

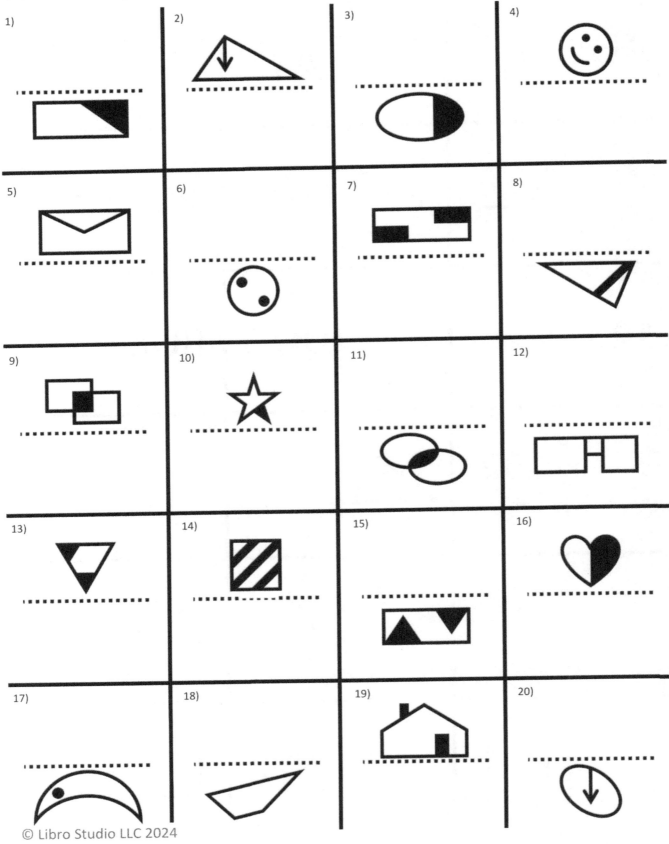

Day 24
Drawing Reflections

Name: _____

Draw what each image will look like when reflected over the line of reflection.

1)

2)

3)

4)

5)

6)

7)

8)

9)

10)

11)

12)

13)

14)

15)

16)

17)

18)

Puzzle

Name: _____

Score:

Identifying Rotations

Rotating a shape turns the shape. The shape remains the same shape even though it's positioned differently.

In each problem below, one of the options on the right is a rotation of the shape that is shown on the left. Find the rotated shape and shade the small letter next to it to indicate your answer.

The other three shapes are different shapes. They are not a rotation of the shape to the left. Look at each of the options carefully and ask yourself, "Is this the same shape as the one to the left, or is this a different shape?"

Example: *Shade option A, B, C or D to indicate which shape is the same as the shape to the left but rotated.*

 | 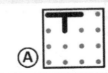 Ⓐ Ⓑ 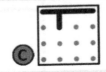 Ⓒ  Ⓓ

Shade option A, B, C or D to indicate which shape is the same as the shape to the left but rotated.

1) Ⓐ 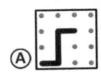 Ⓑ 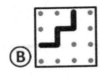 Ⓒ 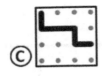 Ⓓ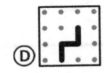

2) Ⓐ 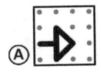 Ⓑ Ⓒ  Ⓓ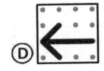

3) Ⓐ  Ⓑ 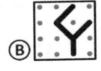 Ⓒ  Ⓓ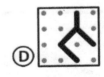

4) Ⓐ  Ⓑ Ⓒ 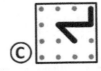 Ⓓ

5) Ⓐ Ⓑ Ⓒ Ⓓ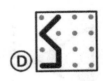

6) Ⓐ  Ⓑ 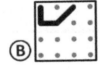 Ⓒ Ⓓ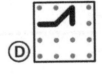

7) Ⓐ Ⓑ 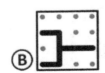 Ⓒ Ⓓ

Day 26
Rotations

Name: _____

Shade option A, B, C or D to indicate which shape is the same as the shape to the left but rotated.

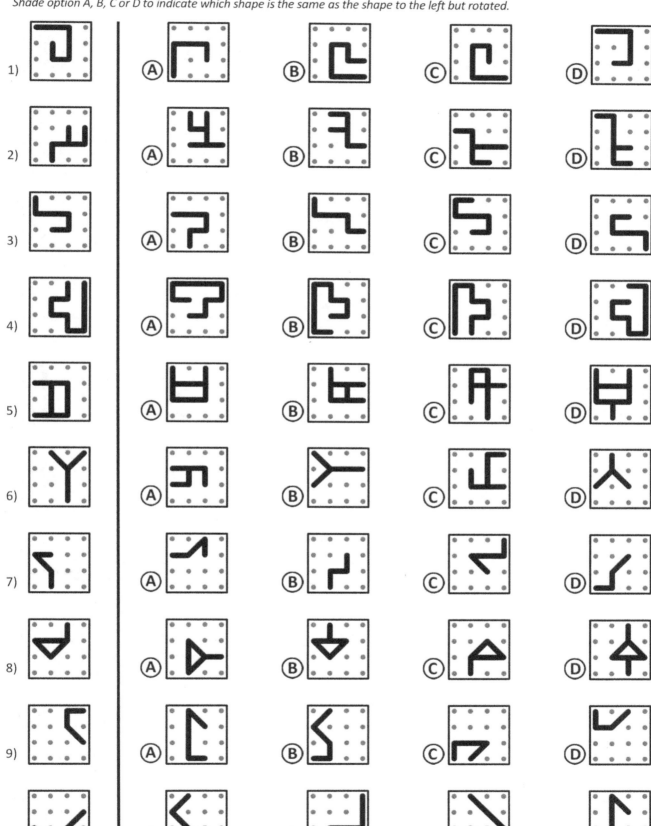

Day 27
Rotations

Name: _____

Score:

Shade option A, B, C or D to indicate which shape is the same as the shape to the left but rotated.

1)  A  B  C  D

2)  A  B 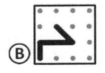 C 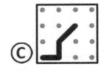 D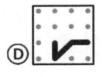

3) A  B  C D

4) A  B C  D

5) A  B  C  D

6) A 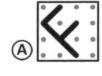 B  C 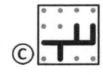 D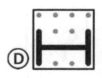

7) A 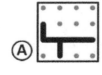 B  C  D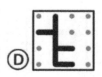

8) A 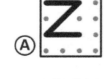 B  C  D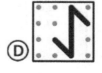

9) A B  C 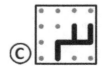 D

10) A B C D

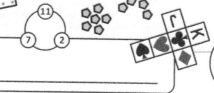

Name: _____

Score:

Shade option A, B, C or D to indicate which shape is the same as the shape to the left but rotated.

1) 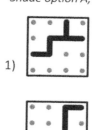   (A) 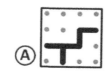   (B) 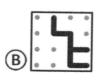   (C) 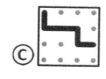   (D)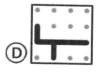

2)   (A) 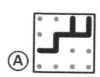   (B)    (C) 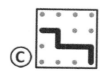   (D)

3)   (A) 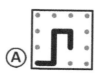   (B) 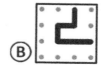   (C)    (D)

4)   (A)    (B) 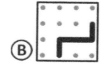   (C) 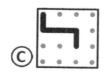   (D)

5) 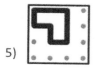   (A)    (B)    (C) 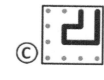   (D)

6)   (A) 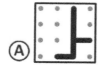   (B)   (C)   (D)

7)   (A)    (B)   (C)    (D)

8) 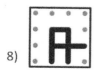   (A) 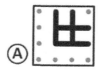   (B)   (C) 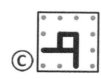   (D)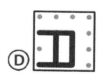

9)   (A)   (B)    (C)   (D)

10)   (A) 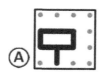   (B) 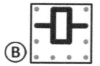   (C) 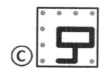   (D)

90° Rotations

A 90° rotation is a quarter turn. The turn can be a **clockwise** turn (to the right) or a **counterclockwise** turn (to the left). A 90° clockwise rotation is not the same as a 90° counterclockwise rotation. The direction of the rotation makes a difference.

Examples:

Original Image:	**90° Clockwise** Rotation:	**90° Counterclockwise** Rotation:

*The images below were rotated 90°. Circle **clockwise** or **counterclockwise** to indicate the direction each image was rotated.*

Before	*After*		*Before*	*After*	
1)		Clockwise / Counterclockwise	7)		Clockwise / Counterclockwise
2)		Clockwise / Counterclockwise	8)		Clockwise / Counterclockwise
3)		Clockwise / Counterclockwise	9)		Clockwise / Counterclockwise
4)		Clockwise / Counterclockwise	10)		Clockwise / Counterclockwise
5)		Clockwise / Counterclockwise	11)		Clockwise / Counterclockwise
6)		Clockwise / Counterclockwise	12)		Clockwise / Counterclockwise

180° Rotations

A 180° rotation is a half turn. The turn can be a **clockwise** turn (to the right) or a **counterclockwise** turn (to the left). A 180° rotation is unique because a 180° clockwise rotation will leave the object in the same position as a 180° counterclockwise rotation and vice versa. Look at the examples below. The 180° rotations look the same.

Examples:

Original Image:	180° Clockwise Rotation:	180° Counterclockwise Rotation:

The images below were either rotated 90° or 180°. Circle an option to indicate which type of rotation it is.

Before **After**

1)
- 90° Clockwise
- 90° Counterclockwise
- 180°

2)
- 90° Clockwise
- 90° Counterclockwise
- 180°

3) J
- 90° Clockwise
- 90° Counterclockwise
- 180°

4)
- 90° Clockwise
- 90° Counterclockwise
- 180°

5) R
- 90° Clockwise
- 90° Counterclockwise
- 180°

6)
- 90° Clockwise
- 90° Counterclockwise
- 180°

Before **After**

7) P d
- 90° Clockwise
- 90° Counterclockwise
- 180°

8)
- 90° Clockwise
- 90° Counterclockwise
- 180°

9)
- 90° Clockwise
- 90° Counterclockwise
- 180°

10) L
- 90° Clockwise
- 90° Counterclockwise
- 180°

11)
- 90° Clockwise
- 90° Counterclockwise
- 180°

12) G G
- 90° Clockwise
- 90° Counterclockwise
- 180°

Puzzle

Name: _____

Score:

Shade A, B, C to indicate what each shape to the left would look like if rotated as described.

1) **Rotated 90° Counterclockwise**

Ⓐ   Ⓑ 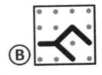 Ⓒ

2) **Rotated 90° Clockwise**

Ⓐ 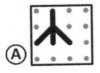 Ⓑ  Ⓒ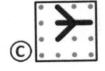

3) **Rotated 180°**

Ⓐ  Ⓑ  Ⓒ

4) **Rotated 90° Clockwise**

Ⓐ   Ⓑ 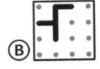 Ⓒ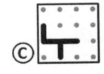

5) **Rotated 90° Counterclockwise**

Ⓐ   Ⓑ  Ⓒ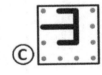

6) **Rotated 180°**

Ⓐ   Ⓑ  Ⓒ

7) **Rotated 90° Counterclockwise**

Ⓐ   Ⓑ  Ⓒ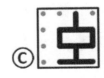

8) **Rotated 180°**

Ⓐ  Ⓑ 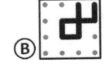 Ⓒ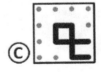

9) **Rotated 90° Clockwise**

Ⓐ  Ⓑ  Ⓒ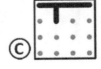

10) **Rotated 90° Counterclockwise**

Ⓐ  Ⓑ  Ⓒ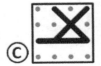

Name: _____

Score:

Shade A, B, C to indicate what each shape to the left would look like if rotated as described.

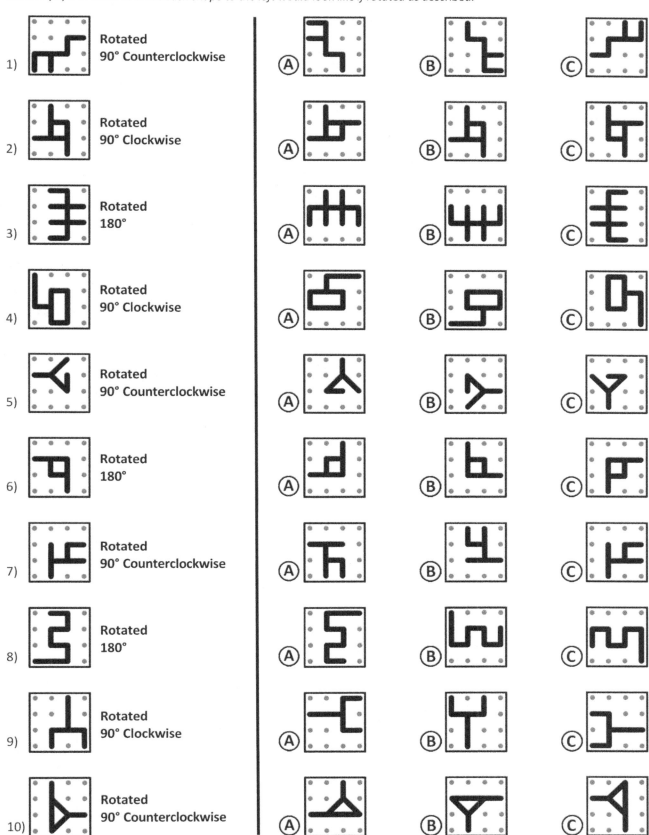

1) Rotated 90° Counterclockwise

2) Rotated 90° Clockwise

3) Rotated 180°

4) Rotated 90° Clockwise

5) Rotated 90° Counterclockwise

6) Rotated 180°

7) Rotated 90° Counterclockwise

8) Rotated 180°

9) Rotated 90° Clockwise

10) Rotated 90° Counterclockwise

You Draw the Rotation

In the previous pages, the rotations were drawn for you. Now, you'll be shown an image and you will need to draw what that image will look like once it's rotated. Pay attention to what type of rotation is supposed to be performed. *Is it a 90° or 180° rotation? Is the rotation clockwise or counterclockwise?*

Helpful Tips:
1. Imagine what the rotation will look like before you begin to draw.
2. Use a pencil to draw so you can erase mistakes.
3. Draw your shapes lightly. Darken the shapes after they look the way you want.

Draw how each shape will look after the rotation is performed.

90° Clockwise Rotations

Before	*After*
1)	
2)	
3)	
4)	
5)	
6)	
7)	

90° Counterclockwise Rotations

Before	*After*
8)	
9)	
10)	
11)	
12)	
13)	
14)	

180° Rotations

Before	*After*
15)	
16)	
17)	
18)	
19)	
20)	
21)	

Name: _____

Score: ___

Draw how each shape will look after the rotation is performed.

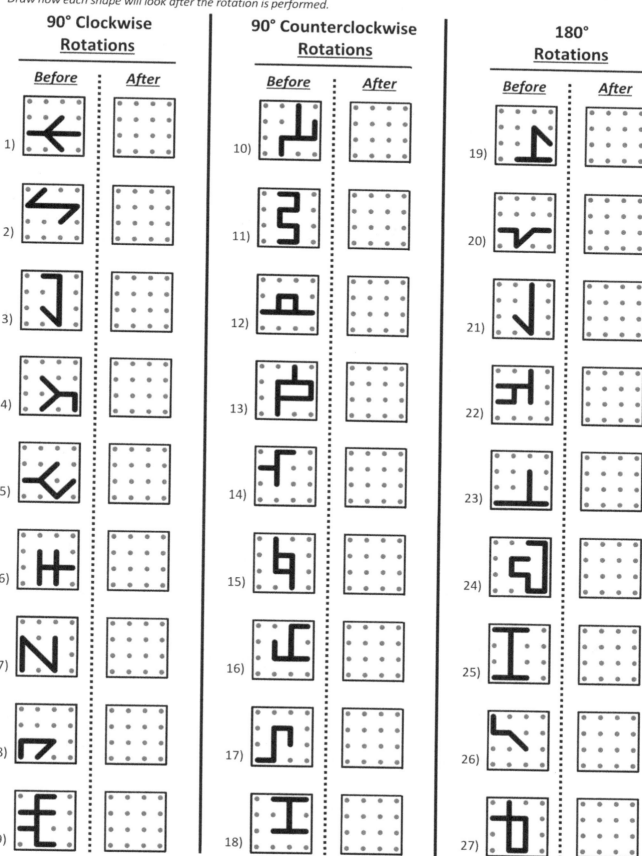

90° Clockwise Rotations

Before — After

1)
2)
3)
4)
5)
6)
7)
8)
9)

90° Counterclockwise Rotations

Before — After

10)
11)
12)
13)
14)
15)
16)
17)
18)

180° Rotations

Before — After

19)
20)
21)
22)
23)
24)
25)
26)
27)

Day 35
Rotations

Name: _____

Score:

Draw how each shape will look after the rotation is performed.

90° Clockwise Rotations

Before	After
1)	
2)	
3)	
4)	
5)	
6)	
7)	
8)	
9)	

90° Counterclockwise Rotations

Before	After
10)	
11)	
12)	
13)	
14)	
15)	
16)	
17)	
18)	

180° Rotations

Before	After
19)	
20)	
21)	
22)	
23)	
24)	
25)	
26)	
27)	

Day 36
Rotations

Name: _____

Score:

Draw how each shape will look after the rotation is performed.

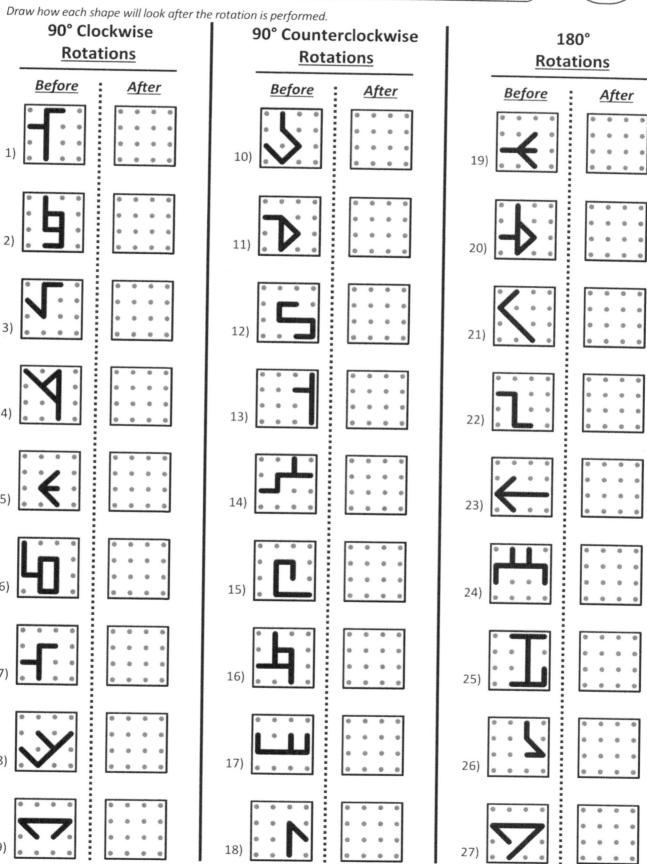

90° Clockwise Rotations

Before	After
1)	
2)	
3)	
4)	
5)	
6)	
7)	
8)	
9)	

90° Counterclockwise Rotations

Before	After
10)	
11)	
12)	
13)	
14)	
15)	
16)	
17)	
18)	

180° Rotations

Before	After
19)	
20)	
21)	
22)	
23)	
24)	
25)	
26)	
27)	

Addition Pyramids

A **number pyramid** is a pyramid of numbers that follows a rule. In an **addition pyramid**, <u>the rule is that each block of the pyramid is the sum of the two blocks below it</u>.

The base blocks of a number pyramid do not have any blocks below them, but the second row of blocks and higher will have blocks below them. To find an unknown number in the pyramid, add the numbers from the two blocks below it.

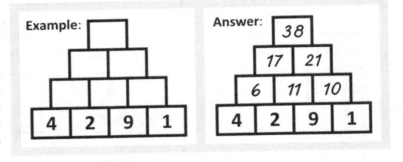

Example:

4	2	9	1

Answer:

	38		
	17	21	
6	11	10	
4	2	9	1

Complete the addition pyramids by calculating the unknown numbers and writing them in the blank blocks.

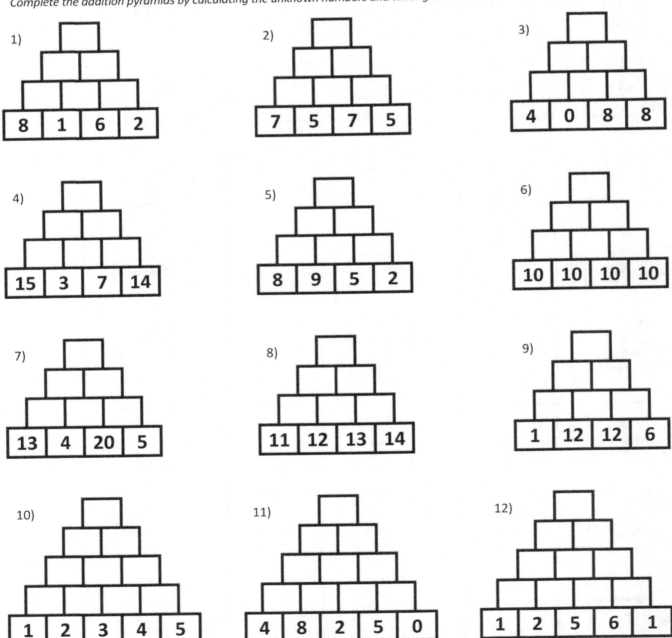

1)

8	1	6	2

2)

7	5	7	5

3)

4	0	8	8

4)

15	3	7	14

5)

8	9	5	2

6)

10	10	10	10

7)

13	4	20	5

8)

11	12	13	14

9)

1	12	12	6

10)

1	2	3	4	5

11)

4	8	2	5	0

12)

1	2	5	6	1

Day 38

Addition Pyramids

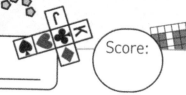

Name: _____

Score:

Complete the addition pyramids by calculating the unknown numbers and writing them in the blank blocks.

1)

5	2	23	1	3

2)

5	5	5	3	8	1	6	2

3)

4	9	1	3	10	7

4)

6	1	4	0	0	0	12	7

5)

2	0	6	13	7	4

6)

3	2	3	4	3	2	3	4

Name: _____

Design Your Own: *Write your own numbers in the row of base blocks, then calculate the numbers for the rest of the blocks.*

1)
2)
3)
4)
5)
6)

Name: _____

Score:

Addition Pyramid: Top to Bottom

Number pyramids do not always have known numbers at their base. Sometimes, known numbers are scattered across the number pyramid, and you need to calculate unknown numbers from top to bottom.

With addition pyramids, you add two blocks to find the number above them. This means subtraction can be used to find a missing number below a block.

An example is shown to the right, and steps to calculate the unknown numbers are shown below. <u>Addition pyramids often have many different ways they can be solved</u>. Even this example can be solved using different steps.

Example:

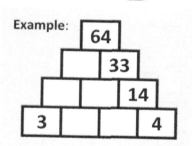

Step 1:
64 − 33 = 31
14 − 4 = 10

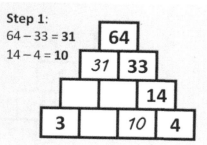

Step 2:
33 − 14 = 19

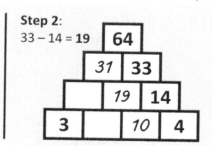

Step 3:
31 − 19 = 12
12 − 3 = 9

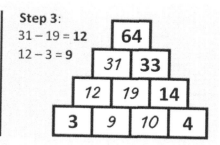

Complete the addition pyramids by calculating the unknown numbers and writing them in the blank blocks.

1)
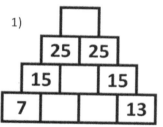

2)
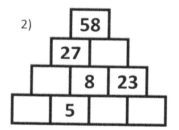

3)
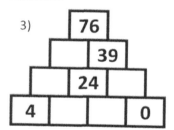

4)
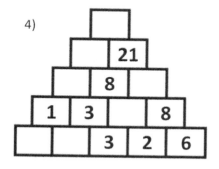

5)
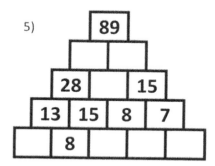

6)
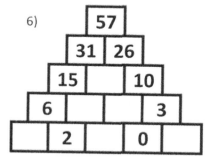

7)
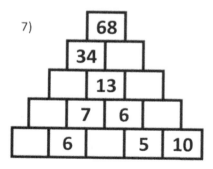

8)
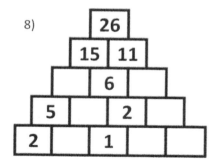

9)
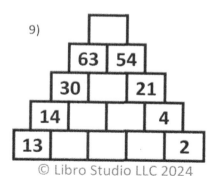

Puzzle Puzzle

Name: _____

Score:

Complete the addition pyramids by calculating the unknown numbers and writing them in the blank blocks.

1)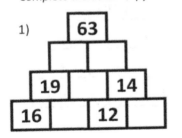

2)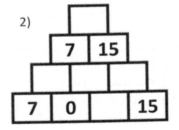

3)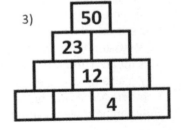

4)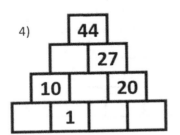

5)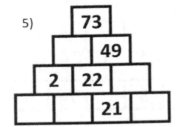

6)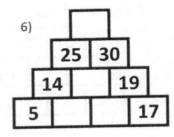

7)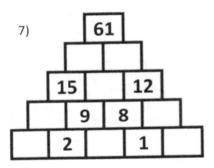

8)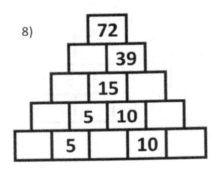

9)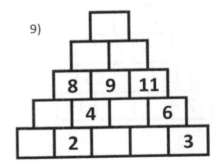

10)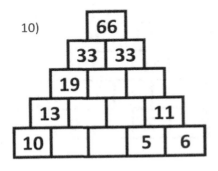

11)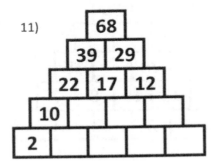

12)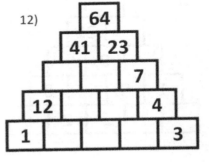

13)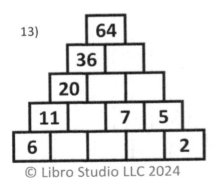

14)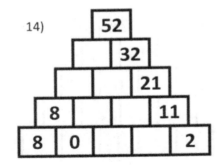

15)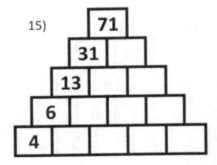

Day 42

Addition Pyramids

Name: _____

Score:

Complete the addition pyramids by calculating the unknown numbers and writing them in the blank blocks.

Puzzle

Name: _____

Complete the addition pyramids by calculating the unknown numbers and writing them in the blank blocks.

1)

| | |
| 54 | 45 |

| | | |
| 3 | 11 | 3 |

2)

506

125

73

21 | 22

23 | 13

11 | 8 | 4 | 8

5 | 6 | 1 | 4

3)

206

123

36

21 | 13 | 5

3 | 3

4)

148

74

14 | 9 | 8 | 9

9

6 | 3

4

5)

187

102

23

7 | 10 | 18 | 11

11

6)

506

253

119

52

21

8

3

1

Name: _____

Score:

Design Your Own: *Create addition pyramid puzzles by writing numbers in some blocks and leaving other blocks blank. Plan your pyramids carefully to ensure that they can be solved.*

1)

2)

3)

4)

5)

6)

Day 45
Number Patterns

Puzzle
Puzzle

Name: _____

Score:

Number Patterns Review

Like other patterns, number patterns are created by a repetitive sequence that does not change. So, a **pattern rule** can be used to describe the sequence. The rule can also be used to calculate other numbers in the pattern.

Finding the Common Difference

Don't know what a **common difference** is? It may be helpful for you to review book 1, shown to the right. Otherwise, a quick explanation is that the common difference is the amount by which each term in the number pattern increases or decreases.

If the pattern is 2, 4, 6, 8, 10…, then the common difference is 2. Since the pattern is increasing by 2, this is a **growth pattern** and the rule for the pattern is "**Add 2**".

If the pattern is 11, 9, 7, 5, 3…, then the common difference is still 2. In this case, the pattern is decreasing by 2, so it is a **decreasing pattern** and the rule for the pattern is "**Subtract 2**".

Calculate the common difference for each number pattern and use that information to **write the pattern rule**.

61, 57, 53, 49, 45, _41_, _37_ …
What's the pattern's rule?
Subtract 4

1) **14, 18, 22, 26, 30,____, ____…**
What's the pattern's rule?

2) **40, 45, 50, 55, 60,____, ____…**
What's the pattern's rule?

3) **55, 54, 53, 52, 51,____, ____…**
What's the pattern's rule?

4) **80, 74, 68, 62, 56,____, ____…**
What's the pattern's rule?

5) **35, 33, 31, 29, 27,____, ____…**
What's the pattern's rule?

6) **62, 65, 68, 71, 74,____, ____…**
What's the pattern's rule?

7) **13, 23, 33, 43, 53,____, ____…**
What's the pattern's rule?

8) **54, 46, 38, 30, 22,____, ____…**
What's the pattern's rule?

9) **85, 87, 89, 91, 93,____, ____…**
What's the pattern's rule?

10) **48, 45, 42, 39, 36,____, ____…**
What's the pattern's rule?

11) **48, 54, 60, 66, 72,____, ____…**
What's the pattern's rule?

12) **64, 69, 74, 79, 84,____, ____…**
What's the pattern's rule?

13) **70, 59, 48, 37, 26,____, ____…**
What's the pattern's rule?

Geometric Sequences

In the previous problems, the number patterns had a common difference that involved addition or subtraction. These types of number patterns are called **arithmetic sequences**.

Today, a new type of number pattern will be introduced. They are called **geometric sequences**. Geometric sequences do not have a common difference. Instead, they have a **common ratio**. A common ratio is similar to a common difference, except a common ratio involves <u>multiplication or division</u>, instead of addition or subtraction.

Common Difference vs. Common Ratio

When a number pattern has a common difference, the difference between each consecutive term remains the same. The difference between terms is consistent from one term to the next. The sequence either grows at a constant rate (when the rule uses addition), or it decreases at a constant rate (when the rule uses subtraction).

When a number pattern has a common ratio, the difference between each consecutive term will not remain the same. There is no common difference. The difference between the terms will change from one set of terms to the next. Multiplying numbers larger than one will cause the number sequence to grow at a faster and faster rate as the sequence continues and division will cause the number sequence to decrease at a slower and slower rate.

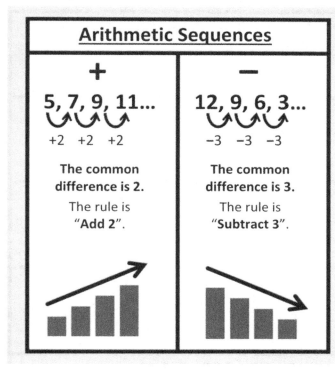

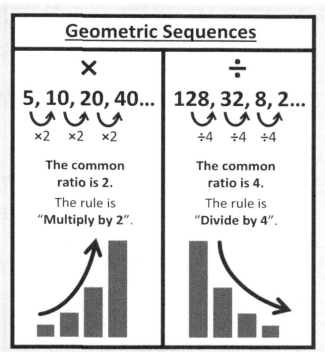

Circle "A" if the sequence is an arithmetic sequence or circle "G" if the sequence is a geometric sequence.

1) **4, 8, 16, 32, 64…** A *or* G	2) **3, 6, 9, 12, 15…** A *or* G
3) **56, 51, 46, 41, 36…** A *or* G	4) **1,024, 256, 32, 16, 4…** A *or* G
5) **80, 70, 60, 50, 40…** A *or* G	6) **7, 14, 28, 56, 112…** A *or* G
7) **20, 40, 60, 80, 100…** A *or* G	8) **400, 200, 100, 50…** A *or* G
9) **4, 12, 36, 108, 324…** A *or* G	10) **250, 225, 200, 175…** A *or* G

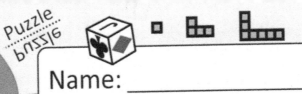
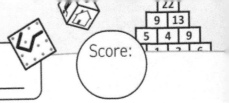
Geometric Sequence Rules

Finding the pattern rule for a geometric sequence is similar to finding the pattern rule for arithmetic sequences. Look at two consecutive terms in the sequence. Divide the larger term by the smaller term. This will determine the common ratio. If it is a growing pattern, each term is being multiplied by the common ratio. If it is a decreasing pattern, each ratio is being divided by the common ratio. (Reviewing the chart on the previous page may be helpful.)

Calculators

Learning multiplication and division is not the goal of this lesson. The main goal is to learn how to calculate the common ratio and determine a pattern's rule. Ask a teacher if a calculator may be used.

Calculate the common ratio for each geometric sequence and use that information to **write the pattern rule**.

1) **4,000, 2,000, 1,000, 500…** _What's the pattern's rule?_	2) **10, 100, 1,000, 10,000…** _What's the pattern's rule?_
3) **6, 12, 24, 48, 96…** _What's the pattern's rule?_	4) **1,215, 405, 135, 45…** _What's the pattern's rule?_
5) **2,500, 500, 100, 20…** _What's the pattern's rule?_	6) **9, 18, 36, 72, 144…** _What's the pattern's rule?_
7) **16,000, 4,000, 1,000, 250…** _What's the pattern's rule?_	8) **10,000, 5,000, 2,500, 1,250…** _What's the pattern's rule?_
9) **30, 150, 750, 3,750…** _What's the pattern's rule?_	10) **5,103, 1,701, 567, 189…** _What's the pattern's rule?_
11) **6,144, 1,536, 384, 96…** _What's the pattern's rule?_	12) **15, 75, 375, 1,875…** _What's the pattern's rule?_
13) **3,888, 648, 108, 18…** _What's the pattern's rule?_	14) **50,000, 5,000, 500, 50…** _What's the pattern's rule?_
15) **45, 135, 405, 1,215…** _What's the pattern's rule?_	16) **68, 136, 272, 544…** _What's the pattern's rule?_

Name: _____

Score:

What Comes Next in the Geometric Sequence?

Once a number pattern's rule is determined that rule can be used to calculate what numbers come next in the sequence. Apply the rule to the last known number in the sequence. It will result in the next number of the sequence.

Example 1: <u>Growing</u> Geometric Sequence

9, 36, 144, 576, _____, _____ …

The Rule: Multiply by 4

Answer 1:

9, 36, 144, 576, <u>2,304</u>, <u>9,216</u> …

(576 × 4 = **2,304** and 2,304 × 4 = **9,216**)

Example 2: <u>Decreasing</u> Geometric Sequence

704, 352, 176, 88, _____, _____ …

The Rule: Divide by 2

Answer 2:

704, 352, 176, 88, <u>44</u>, <u>22</u> …

(88 ÷ 2 = **44** and 44 ÷ 2 = **22**)

Determine the pattern's rule and use it to calculate the next two numbers in the sequence.

1) *What's the pattern's rule?*

8,748, 2,916, 972, 324…

_____, _____

2) *What's the pattern's rule?*

21,875, 4,375, 875, 175…

_____, _____

3) *What's the pattern's rule?*

12, 48, 192, 768…

_____, _____

4) *What's the pattern's rule?*

39, 117, 351, 1,053…

_____, _____

5) *What's the pattern's rule?*

7,680, 3,840, 1,920, 960…

_____, _____

6) *What's the pattern's rule?*

8, 40, 200, 1,000…

_____, _____

7) *What's the pattern's rule?*

92, 184, 368, 736…

_____, _____

8) *What's the pattern's rule?*

14,336, 3,584, 896, 224…

_____, _____

9) *What's the pattern's rule?*

42, 252, 1,512, 9,072…

_____, _____

10) *What's the pattern's rule?*

3,888, 1,296, 432, 144…

_____, _____

11) *What's the pattern's rule?*

1,664, 832, 416, 208…

_____, _____

12) *What's the pattern's rule?*

51, 153, 459, 1,377…

_____, _____

Name: _____

Score:

Determine the pattern rule, then use the rule to calculate the next two numbers in the sequence.

1) What's the pattern's rule?

30, 150, 750, 3,750...

_____, _____

2) What's the pattern's rule?

1,216, 608, 304, 152...

_____, _____

3) What's the pattern's rule?

3, 24, 192, 1,536...

_____, _____

4) What's the pattern's rule?

54,432, 9,072, 1,512, 252...

_____, _____

5) What's the pattern's rule?

36,864, 9,216, 2,304, 576...

_____, _____

6) What's the pattern's rule?

40, 80, 160, 320...

_____, _____

7) What's the pattern's rule?

24,057, 8,019, 2,673, 891...

_____, _____

8) What's the pattern's rule?

52, 208, 832, 3,328...

_____, _____

9) What's the pattern's rule?

42, 252, 1,512, 9,072...

_____, _____

10) What's the pattern's rule?

93,750 , 18,750, 3,750, 750...

_____, _____

11) What's the pattern's rule?

2,688 , 1,344, 672, 336...

_____, _____

12) What's the pattern's rule?

48, 144, 432, 1,296...

_____, _____

13) What's the pattern's rule?

16,384, 4,096, 1,024, 256...

_____, _____

14) What's the pattern's rule?

3, 30, 300, 3,000...

_____, _____

15) What's the pattern's rule?

50,421, 7,203, 1,029, 147...

_____, _____

16) What's the pattern's rule?

52, 104, 208, 416 ...

_____, _____

17) What's the pattern's rule?

39, 117, 351, 1,053...

_____, _____

18) What's the pattern's rule?

3,200, 1,600, 800, 400...

_____, _____

Name: _____

Score:

What Comes Next in Arithmetic and Geometric Sequences?

The sequences below may be arithmetic or geometric. This means the pattern's rule may involve addition, subtraction, multiplication, or division. Determine each pattern's rule, then find the next two numbers in the sequence.

Determine the pattern rule, then use the rule to calculate the next two numbers in the sequence.

1) *What's the pattern's rule?*

   51, 74, 97, 120…

   _____ , _____

2) *What's the pattern's rule?*

   58, 116, 232, 464…

   _____ , _____

3) *What's the pattern's rule?*

   18,225, 6,075, 2,025, 675…

   _____ , _____

4) *What's the pattern's rule?*

   527, 492, 457, 422…

   _____ , _____

5) *What's the pattern's rule?*

   5,248, 2,624, 1,312, 656…

   _____ , _____

6) *What's the pattern's rule?*

   902, 970, 1,038, 1,106…

   _____ , _____

7) *What's the pattern's rule?*

   250,000, 50,000, 10,000, 2,000…

   _____ , _____

8) *What's the pattern's rule?*

   4,267, 4,142, 4,017, 3,892…

   _____ , _____

9) *What's the pattern's rule?*

   68, 272, 1,088, 4,352…

   _____ , _____

10) *What's the pattern's rule?*

   41,553, 13,851, 4,617, 1,539…

   _____ , _____

11) *What's the pattern's rule?*

   10,182, 10,135, 10,088, 10,041…

   _____ , _____

12) *What's the pattern's rule?*

   2,359, 2,964, 3,569, 4,174…

   _____ , _____

13) *What's the pattern's rule?*

   5,504, 2,752, 1,376, 688…

   _____ , _____

14) *What's the pattern's rule?*

   9,892, 8,692, 7,492, 6,292…

   _____ , _____

15) *What's the pattern's rule?*

   60, 300, 1,500, 7,500…

   _____ , _____

16) *What's the pattern's rule?*

   38,880, 6,480, 1,080, 180…

   _____ , _____

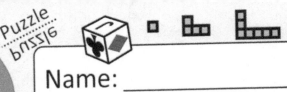

Puzzle

Name: _____

Score:

Determine the pattern rule, then use the rule to calculate the next two numbers in the sequence.

1) *What's the pattern's rule?*

   1,248, 1,153, 1,058, 963...

   _____, _____

2) *What's the pattern's rule?*

   34, 102, 306, 918...

   _____, _____

3) *What's the pattern's rule?*

   3,780, 4,032, 4,284, 4,536...

   _____, _____

4) *What's the pattern's rule?*

   12,381, 11,197, 10,013, 8,829...

   _____, _____

5) *What's the pattern's rule?*

   6,784, 3,392, 1,696, 848...

   _____, _____

6) *What's the pattern's rule?*

   27,648, 6,912, 1,728, 432...

   _____, _____

7) *What's the pattern's rule?*

   19, 95, 475, 2,375...

   _____, _____

8) *What's the pattern's rule?*

   3,068, 5,154, 7,240, 9,326...

   _____, _____

9) *What's the pattern's rule?*

   218, 436, 872, 1,744...

   _____, _____

10) *What's the pattern's rule?*

   627, 1,254, 2,508, 5,016...

   _____, _____

11) *What's the pattern's rule?*

   17,254, 16,672, 16,090, 15,508...

   _____, _____

12) *What's the pattern's rule?*

   3,561, 3,955, 4,349, 4,743...

   _____, _____

13) *What's the pattern's rule?*

   26,244 , 8,748, 2,916, 972...

   _____, _____

14) *What's the pattern's rule?*

   583, 5,253, 9,923, 14,593...

   _____, _____

15) *What's the pattern's rule?*

   60, 240, 960, 3,840...

   _____, _____

16) *What's the pattern's rule?*

   20,351, 16,879, 13,407, 9,935...

   _____, _____

17) *What's the pattern's rule?*

   65,625, 13,125, 2,625, 525...

   _____, _____

18) *What's the pattern's rule?*

   32,416, 37,024, 41,632, 46,240...

   _____, _____

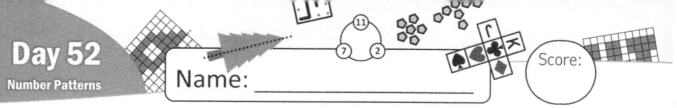

Name: _____

Score:

Calculate the Missing Numbers

Instead of finding the numbers that come next in a number pattern, see if you can use your skills to find the missing numbers within a pattern too. Calculate the common difference or common ratio, then determine the rule. Once you know the rule for the pattern, use it to calculate the missing numbers.

Determine the pattern rule, then use the rule to calculate the missing numbers in the sequence.

1) 782, 846, _____, 974, _____, 1,102...

2) _____, 150, 300 , 600, _____, 2,400...

3) 48, _____, 432, 1,296, 3,888, _____...

4) _____, 4,457, _____, 4,353, 4,301, 4,249...

5) 45, 225, _____, 5,625, _____, 140,625...

6) 2,351, 2,177, _____, _____, 1,655, 1,481...

7) _____, 1,504, 752, 376, 188, _____...

8) 7,393, _____, 8,451, _____, 9,509, 10,038...

9) _____, _____, 5,568, 1,392, 348, 87...

10) _____, 56, 392, 2,744, _____, 134,456...

11) 11,130, 10,147, 9,164, _____, _____, 6,215...

12) _____, 959, 885, 811, 737, _____...

13) 2,016, _____, 504, 252, _____, 63...

Puzzle

Name: _____

Score:

Determine the pattern rule, then use the rule to calculate the missing numbers in the sequence.

1) 6,510, _____, 5,814, 5,466, 5,118, _____ ...

2) _____, 60, _____, 6,000, 60,000, 600,000...

3) 6,705, 7,487, _____, 9,051, _____, 10,615...

4) _____, 378, 1,134, 3,402, 10,206, _____ ...

5) _____, 8,960, 2,240, 560, _____, 35...

6) 12,188, _____, 8,062, 5,999, 3,936, _____ ...

7) _____, 706, 1,412, 2,824, 5,648, _____ ...

8) 6,419, _____, 10,227, _____, 14,035, 15,939...

9) 16,281 , _____, 1,809, 603, _____, 67...

10) 5,628, 5,211, _____, 4,377, _____, 3,543...

11) 55, 220, 880, _____, _____, 56,320...

12) _____, _____, 1,141, 1,229, 1,317, 1,405...

13) 30,516, 26,235, _____, _____, 13,392, 9,111...

14) 18,304, 9,152, _____, 2,288, _____, 572...

Name: _____

Score:

Determine the pattern rule, then use the rule to calculate the missing numbers in the sequence.

1) _____, 196, 784, 3,136, 12,544, _____...

2) 40,625, 8125, 1,625, _____, _____, 13...

3) 5,600, 5,249, _____, _____, 4,196, 3,845...

4) 16, _____, 576, 3,456, 20,736, _____...

5) 154, _____, 7,316, _____, 14,478, 18,059...

6) _____, 10,272, 5,136, 2,568, 1,284, _____...

7) _____, _____, 3,087, 3,901, 4,715, 5,529...

8) _____, 363, _____, 3,267, 9,801, 29,403...

9) 10,518, _____, 9,076, 8,355, 7,634, _____...

10) _____, 12,636, _____, 1,404, 468, 156...

11) 62,464, _____, 3,904, 976, 244, _____...

12) _____, 5,702, 8,257, 10,812, 13,367, _____...

13) 586, 1,172, _____, 4,688, _____, 18,752...

14) _____, 801, 712, 623, _____, 445...

Name: _____

Determine the pattern rule, then use the rule to calculate the missing numbers in the sequence.

1) _____, 5,479, 5,287, 5,095, 4,903, _____ ...

2) 21,540, _____, 16,506, 13,989, 11,472, _____ ...

3) 904, 1,808, _____, 7,232, _____, 28,928...

4) _____, 90,000, _____, 900, 90, 9...

5) 87, _____, 2,175, 10,875, _____, 271,875...

6) _____, 4,856, 9,040, 13,224, 17,408, _____ ...

7) _____, 5,632, 1,408 , 352, _____, 22...

8) 8,209, _____, 7,249, _____, 6,289, 5,809...

9) 145, 435, _____, _____, 11,745, 35,235...

10) 9,561, 8,320, _____, 5,838, _____, 3,356...

11) _____, _____, 3,581, 4,194, 4,807, 5,420...

12) 33,920, 16,960, 8,480, _____, _____, 1,060...

13) 9, 72, _____, 4,608, _____, 294,912...

14) 6,218, _____, 17,656, 23,375, 29,094, _____ ...

Day 56
Number Patterns

Name: _____

Score:

Determine the pattern rule, then use the rule to calculate the missing numbers in the sequence.

1) _____, 171, 513, 1,539, 4,617, _____...

2) 10,578 _____, 8,702, _____, 6,826, 5,888...

3) 43,008, 10,752, _____, _____, 168, 42...

4) 2,571, 3,874 , 5,177, _____, _____, 9,086 ...

5) 8,195, 8,907, _____, 10,331, _____, 11,755...

6) 7,712, 3,856, _____, 964, _____, 241...

7) 23,480, _____, 19,312, _____, 15,144 , 13,060...

8) 17, _____, 425, 2,125, _____, 53,125...

9) _____, _____, 2,916, 972, 324, 108 ...

10) 671, _____, 2,684, 5,368, 10,736, _____...

11) _____, 7,297, 6,734, 6,171, 5,608, _____...

12) 20,412, 6,804, _____, 756, _____, 84...

13) 2,462, _____, 3,946, 4,688, 5,430, _____...

14) _____, 114, _____, 4,104, 24,624, 147,744...

Quadratic Sequences

Remember how arithmetic sequences have a common difference? (Refer back to Days 45 and 46 if it helps). It's called a common difference because the difference between any two terms remains the same.

In a **quadratic sequence**, the difference between consecutive terms does not stay the same. The difference between consecutive terms changes by a constant amount. In other words, the difference between consecutive terms creates a new number pattern. This new number pattern is an arithmetic sequence, for which a common difference can be found.

With quadratic sequences, the **first difference** between consecutive terms will form an arithmetic sequence, and the **second difference** will be a common difference (all the differences between the terms will be the same amount).

Example 1: 3, 8, 15, 24, 35…

3, 8, 15, 24, 35…

First Difference   +5 +7 +9 +11

Second Difference   +2 +2 +2

The <u>second difference</u> has a **common difference of 2**.

The pattern's <u>rule</u> for the <u>first difference</u> is **"add 2"**.

Example 2: 80, 78, 73, 65, 54…

80, 78, 73, 65, 54…

First Difference   −2 −5 −8 −11

Second Difference   −3 −3 −3

The <u>second difference</u> has a **common difference of 3**.

The pattern's <u>rule</u> for the <u>first difference</u> is **"subtract 3"**.

Finding the Pattern's Rule for the First Difference

Writing the first and second differences makes it easier to visualize and understand quadratic sequences. In the examples above, arrows were used to represent the difference from one term to the next. Many people prefer to use lines to organize the first and second differences instead. Lines are simple to use. The first problem below uses lines instead of arrows. You can choose to write the first and second differences whichever way you like.

*Find the pattern's **rule for the first difference**.*

Example) *Rule for the first difference:* **Add 3**

2, 6, 13, 23, 36…
+4 +7 +10 +13
+3 +3 +3

1) *Rule for the first difference:*

62, 58, 52, 44, 34…

2) *Rule for the first difference:*

75, 70, 64, 57, 49…

3) *Rule for the first difference:*

10, 30, 49, 67…

4) *Rule for the first difference:*

120, 125, 134, 147, 164…

5) *Rule for the first difference:*

34, 45, 57, 70, 84…

Name: _____

Score:

Quadratic Sequences: Calculating the Next Terms

Once the rule for the first difference is known, it can be used to calculate the next terms in the first difference's sequence, and the terms of the first sequence can be used to calculate the next terms of the quadratic sequence.

Example: *What are the next two terms of the sequence?*

3, 8, 15, 24, 35...

First Difference   +5   +7   +9   +11

Second Difference   +2   +2   +2

Answer: 48, 63

3, 8, 15, 24, 35, 48, 63...

+5   +7   +9   +11   +13   +15

+2   +2   +2   +2   +2

*Find the pattern's **rule for the first difference** and use it to find the **next two terms of the quadratic sequence**.*

1) *Rule for the first difference:*

   14, 17, 25, 38, 56...

   _____ , _____

2) *Rule for the first difference:*

   100, 95, 87, 76, 62...

   _____ , _____

3) *Rule for the first difference:*

   120, 116, 110, 102, 92...

   _____ , _____

4) *Rule for the first difference:*

   132, 133, 135, 138, 142...

   _____ , _____

5) *Rule for the first difference:*

   4, 7, 16, 31, 52...

   _____ , _____

6) *Rule for the first difference:*

   23, 43, 61, 77, 91...

   _____ , _____

7) *Rule for the first difference:*

   100, 92, 85, 79, 74...

   _____ , _____

8) *Rule for the first difference:*

   260, 255, 245, 230...

   _____ , _____

9) *Rule for the first difference:*

   66, 75, 83, 90, 96...

   _____ , _____

10) *Rule for the first difference:*

   322, 328, 336, 346, 358...

   _____ , _____

Puzzle

Name: _____

Score:

Find the pattern's **rule for the first difference** and use it to find the **next two terms of the quadratic sequence**.

1) *Rule for the first difference:*

350, 371, 389, 404, 416...

_____, _____

2) *Rule for the first difference:*

76, 80, 85, 91, 98...

_____, _____

3) *Rule for the first difference:*

448, 442, 430, 412, 388...

_____, _____

4) *Rule for the first difference:*

79, 77, 74, 70, 65...

_____, _____

5) *Rule for the first difference:*

35, 45, 59, 77, 99...

_____, _____

6) *Rule for the first difference:*

67, 78, 91, 106, 123...

_____, _____

7) *Rule for the first difference:*

114, 110, 104, 96, 86...

_____, _____

8) *Rule for the first difference:*

704, 678, 655, 635, 618...

_____, _____

9) *Rule for the first difference:*

37, 82, 122, 157, 187, ...

_____, _____

10) *Rule for the first difference:*

965, 971, 978, 986...

_____, _____

11) *Rule for the first difference:*

675, 635, 602, 576, 557...

_____, _____

12) *Rule for the first difference:*

637, 636, 631, 622, 609...

_____, _____

Name: _____

Score:

Find the pattern's **rule for the first difference** and use it to find the **next two terms of the quadratic sequence**.

1) Rule for the first difference:

411, 402, 394, 387…

_____, _____

2) Rule for the first difference:

200, 202, 208, 218…

_____, _____

3) Rule for the first difference:

124, 146, 166, 184…

_____, _____

4) Rule for the first difference:

511, 526, 551, 586…

_____, _____

5) Rule for the first difference:

280, 380, 477, 571…

_____, _____

6) Rule for the first difference:

89, 85, 80, 74…

_____, _____

7) Rule for the first difference:

794, 782, 766, 746…

_____, _____

8) Rule for the first difference:

665, 673, 683, 695…

_____, _____

9) Rule for the first difference:

365, 323, 286, 254…

_____, _____

10) Rule for the first difference:

576, 570, 558, 540…

_____, _____

11) Rule for the first difference:

101, 108, 123, 146…

_____,

12) Rule for the first difference:

98, 91, 82, 71…

_____, _____

*Find the pattern's **rule for the first difference** and use it to find the **next two terms of the quadratic sequence**.*

1) *Rule for the first difference:*

26, 41, 60, 83...

_____, _____

2) *Rule for the first difference:*

87, 82, 74, 63...

_____, _____

3) *Rule for the first difference:*

15, 40, 67, 96...

_____, _____

4) *Rule for the first difference:*

287, 263, 241, 221...

_____, _____

5) *Rule for the first difference:*

874, 858, 843, 829...

_____, _____

6) *Rule for the first difference:*

651, 642, 628, 609...

_____, _____

7) *Rule for the first difference:*

264, 260, 246, 222...

_____, _____

8) *Rule for the first difference:*

450, 404, 365, 333...

_____, _____

9) *Rule for the first difference:*

42, 39, 35, 30...

_____, _____

10) *Rule for the first difference:*

386, 397, 412, 431...

_____, _____

11) *Rule for the first difference:*

350, 327, 307, 290...

_____, _____

12) *Rule for the first difference:*

656, 653, 648, 641...

_____, _____

Name: _____

Score: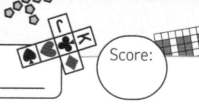

*Find the pattern's **rule for the first difference** and use it to find the **next two terms of the quadratic sequence**.*

1) *Rule for the first difference:*

151, 144, 131, 112…

_____, _____

2) *Rule for the first difference:*

233, 235, 241, 251…

_____, _____

3) *Rule for the first difference:*

341, 350, 368, 395…

_____, _____

4) *Rule for the first difference:*

62, 64, 67, 71…

_____, _____

5) *Rule for the first difference:*

681, 690, 702, 717…

_____, _____

6) *Rule for the first difference:*

543, 541, 534, 522…

_____, _____

7) *Rule for the first difference:*

856, 836, 818, 802…

_____, _____

8) *Rule for the first difference:*

478, 487, 498, 511…

_____, _____

9) *Rule for the first difference:*

42, 67, 89, 108…

_____, _____

10) *Rule for the first difference:*

972, 872, 782, 702…

_____, _____

11) *Rule for the first difference:*

351, 359, 370, 384…

_____, _____

12) *Rule for the first difference:*

640, 580, 525, 475…

_____, _____

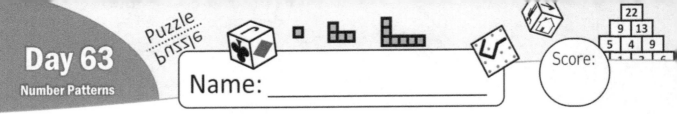

Name: _____

Score:

Mixed Review: Arithmetic, Geometric, and Quadratic Sequences

The number patterns below may be arithmetic, geometric, or quadratic sequences. You will need to identify which type of sequence it is, then use your knowledge of the sequence to calculate the next two terms.

Refer to previous lessons to review each type of sequence. Ask yourself if the number pattern has a <u>constant difference</u> (arithmetic sequence), a <u>constant ratio</u> (geometric sequence), or if the <u>difference changes at a constant rate</u> (quadratic sequence).

Circle **A** *for* **arithmetic,** **G** *for* **geometric,** *and* **Q** *for* **quadratic** *to indicate which type of sequence is shown, then calculate the* **next two terms of the sequence.**

1) **325, 331, 337, 343…** A G Q _____ , _____	2) **782, 777, 770, 761…** A G Q _____ , _____
3) **5, 15, 45, 135…** A G Q _____ , _____	4) **4, 14, 34, 64…** A G Q _____ , _____
5) **768, 746, 724, 702…** A G Q _____ , _____	6) **2,673, 891, 297, 99…** A G Q _____ , _____
7) **2,400, 2,200, 1,900, 1,500…** A G Q _____ , _____	8) **24, 48, 96, 192…** A G Q _____ , _____
9) **135, 160, 190, 225…** A G Q _____ , _____	10) **365, 397, 429, 461…** A G Q _____ , _____

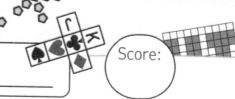

Name: _____

Score:

Circle **A** for **arithmetic**, **G** for **geometric**, and **Q** for **quadratic** to indicate which type of sequence is shown, then calculate the **next two terms of the sequence**.

1) **16, 48, 144, 432…**

A G Q _____ , _____

2) **5,120, 1,280, 320, 80…**

A G Q _____ , _____

3) **249, 306, 363, 420…**

A G Q _____ , _____

4) **308, 320, 335, 353…**

A G Q _____ , _____

5) **781, 766, 751, 736…**

A G Q _____ , _____

6) **245, 225, 207, 191…**

A G Q _____ , _____

7) **6,250, 1,250, 250, 50…**

A G Q _____ , _____

8) **205, 312, 419, 526…**

A G Q _____ , _____

9) **45, 51, 62, 78…**

A G Q _____ , _____

10) **57, 114, 228, 456…**

A G Q _____ , _____

11) **744, 676, 608, 540…**

A G Q _____ , _____

12) **289, 264, 240, 217…**

A G Q _____ , _____

Circle **A** for *arithmetic*, **G** for *geometric*, and **Q** for *quadratic* to indicate which type of sequence is shown, then calculate the **next two terms of the sequence**.

1) **917, 915, 909, 899...**

A G Q _____, _____

2) **472, 455, 438, 421...**

A G Q _____, _____

3) **14, 56, 224, 896...**

A G Q _____, _____

4) **4,860, 1,620, 540, 180...**

A G Q _____, _____

5) **206, 179, 156, 137...**

A G Q _____, _____

6) **613, 647, 681, 715...**

A G Q _____, _____

7) **78, 94, 109, 123...**

A G Q _____, _____

8) **2,336, 1,168, 584, 292...**

A G Q _____, _____

9) **197, 168, 139, 110...**

A G Q _____, _____

10) **127, 220, 313, 406...**

A G Q _____, _____

11) **748, 716, 688, 664...**

A G Q _____, _____

12) **167, 334, 668, 1,336...**

A G Q _____, _____

Name: _____

Score:

2-Step Number Patterns

The previous number patterns were **1-step number patterns**, meaning the rule for these patterns only involved one operation. Today's number patterns are **2-step number patterns**, meaning the pattern's rule will involve two operations.

Using 2-Step Rules

Once a pattern's rule is known, it can be used to calculate the next numbers in the number sequence. When a pattern has a 2-step rule, it's important to <u>perform the steps in order</u>. If the rule is "multiply by 2 and then add 5", the multiplication would need to be done first. Performing the steps backward by adding 5, then multiplying by 2 will result in the wrong numbers being calculated. <u>The order of the steps matters.</u>

Example: *The pattern's rule is to* __**multiply by 2**__ *and then* _____**add 5**_____.

$$3, \ 11, \ 27, \ 59, \ _____, \ _____ \ ...$$

Calculate the **first missing number**:
Step 1: $59 \times 2 = 118$
Step 2: $118 + 5 = 123$

Calculate the **second missing number**:
Step 1: $123 \times 2 = 246$
Step 2: $246 + 5 = 251$

Answer: $3, \ 11, \ 27, \ 59, \ \underline{\ 123 \ }, \ \underline{\ 251 \ } \ ...$

Use the pattern's rule to find the next two numbers in the sequence.

1) *The pattern's rule is to* _____**multiply by 2**_____ *and then* _____**add 3**_____.

5, 13, 29, 61...

_____, _____

2) *The pattern's rule is to* _____**multiply by 2**_____ *and then* _____**subtract 7**_____.

12, 17, 27, 47...

_____, _____

3) *The pattern's rule is to* _____**add 4**_____ *and then* _____**multiply by 2**_____.

5, 18, 44, 96...

_____, _____

4) *The pattern's rule is to* _____**subtract 10**_____ *and then* _____**multiply by 3**_____.

18, 24, 42, 96...

_____, _____

5) *The pattern's rule is to* _____**divide by 2**_____ *and then* _____**add 2,000**_____.

20,000, 12,000, 8,000, 6,000...

_____, _____

6) *The pattern's rule is to* _____**divide by 3**_____ *and then* _____**subtract 7**_____.

3,513, 1,164, 381, 120...

_____, _____

7) *The pattern's rule is to* _____**add 15**_____ *and then* _____**divide by 4**_____.

4,101, 1,029, 261, 69...

_____, _____

8) *The pattern's rule is to* _____**subtract 5**_____ *and then* _____**divide by 2**_____.

955, 475, 235, 115...

_____, _____

Name: _____

Score:

Finding a 2-Step Number Pattern Rule (With Multiplication)

Past lessons required you to find the rule for a number pattern. Those were 1-step patterns though. Today, the goal is to determine the rule for 2-step number patterns and use it to calculate the next two numbers of the pattern.

Determining a 2-step rule often requires trial and error. Use a calculator to assist. Analyze the terms. Test out different operations. Figure out the steps needed to change the value of one term to the value of the next term of the sequence. **(Today's problems will only involve <u>multiplication</u> for one step and <u>addition or subtraction</u> for the other step.)**

When you think you've found the rule, test it out on different consecutive sets of terms. If the rule can be applied to each term to find the next term of the sequence, you've identified the rule. If the steps only work for one or two of the terms but do not work for the rest, then it's not the pattern's rule.

Example: *The pattern's rule is to* _____ *and then* _____ .

        8, 12, 24, 60, _____, _____...

    Trial and error to find the pattern's rule:
- *Is it multiply by 2, and then subtract 4?* (**No**, this only works for the first pair of terms.)
- *Is it add 4?* (**No**, this only works for the first pair of terms.)
- *Is it subtract 4 and then multiply by 3?* (**Yes**, this rule works for each pairs of terms.)

Answer: *The pattern's rule is to* ___**Subtract 4**___ *and then* ___**Multiply by 3**___.

        8, 12, 24, 60, ___**168**___, ___**492**___...

Are You Ready for a Challenge?

Determining the rule for a 2-step problem is usually more difficult than a 1-step problem—but that's not a bad thing. Challenges can be fun. Each problem is like a puzzle. Use your wits and determination to solve each one.

Determine the pattern's 2-step rule.

1) *The pattern's rule is to* _____
   and then _____.
   34, 63, 121, 237, 469...

2) *The pattern's rule is to* _____
   and then _____.
   47, 98, 200, 404, 812...

3) *The pattern's rule is to* _____
   and then _____.
   3, 18, 48, 108, 228...

4) *The pattern's rule is to* _____
   and then _____.
   10, 15, 30, 75, 210...

5) *The pattern's rule is to* _____
   and then _____.
   2, 24, 68, 156, 332...

6) *The pattern's rule is to* _____
   and then _____.
   4, 10, 40, 190, 940...

7) *The pattern's rule is to* _____
   and then _____.
   4, 13, 40, 121, 364...

8) *The pattern's rule is to* _____
   and then _____.
   10, 24, 66, 192, 570...

9) *The pattern's rule is to* _____
   and then _____.
   1, 16, 46, 106, 226...

10) *The pattern's rule is to* _____
    and then _____.
    25, 35, 65, 155, 425...

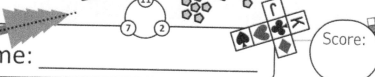

Name: _____

Score: _____

Using a 2-Step Rule (With Multiplication)

You have had practice using a 2-step rule to find the next terms in a sequence. You've had practice using trial and error to find 2-step rules too. Today, the goal is for you to combine these skills by determining the 2-step rule and then using it to find the next terms in the sequence.

You may have noticed that **many of the 2-step rules create quadratic sequences**. Your knowledge of quadratic sequences can also be used to find the next terms in the sequence and check that the 2-step rule you found is correct.

Determine the pattern's 2-step rule and use it to calculate the next two numbers in the sequence.

1) The pattern's rule is to _____ and then _____.

201, 394, 780, 1,552…

_____, _____

2) The pattern's rule is to _____ and then _____.

4, 12, 28, 60…

_____, _____

3) The pattern's rule is to _____ and then _____.

8, 26, 62, 134…

_____, _____

4) The pattern's rule is to _____ and then _____.

10, 12, 18, 36…

_____, _____

5) The pattern's rule is to _____ and then _____.

3, 46, 132, 304…

_____, _____

6) The pattern's rule is to _____ and then _____.

6, 14, 30, 62…

_____, _____

7) The pattern's rule is to _____ and then _____.

30, 35, 45, 65, 105, 185…

_____, _____

8) The pattern's rule is to _____ and then _____.

22, 39, 73, 141…

_____, _____

9) The pattern's rule is to _____ and then _____.

1, 8, 36, 148, 596…

_____, _____

10) The pattern's rule is to _____ and then _____.

150, 200, 300, 500, 900…

_____, _____

11) The pattern's rule is to _____ and then _____.

1, 8, 29, 92, 281…

_____, _____

12) The pattern's rule is to _____ and then _____.

50, 120, 330, 960, 2,850…

_____, _____

Puzzle

Name: _____

Score:

Using a 2-Step Rule (With Division)

2-Step rules are not easy to find. That's why previous problems only involved multiplication with one other operation. Today's problems will include **division in one of the steps,** and then use addition or subtraction in the other step.

Determine the pattern's 2-step rule and use it to calculate the next two numbers in the sequence.

1) The pattern's rule is to _____ and then _____.

694, 342, 166, 78…

_____, _____

2) The pattern's rule is to _____ and then _____.

8,070, 4,038, 2,022, 1,014…

_____, _____

3) The pattern's rule is to _____ and then _____.

4,377, 1,461, 489, 165…

_____, _____

4) The pattern's rule is to _____ and then _____.

21,832, 5,448, 1,352, 328…

_____, _____

5) The pattern's rule is to _____ and then _____.

11,598, 5,774, 2,862, 1,406…

_____, _____

6) The pattern's rule is to _____ and then _____.

74,544, 18,736, 4,784, 1,296…

_____, _____

7) The pattern's rule is to _____ and then _____.

620, 215, 80, 35…

_____, _____

8) The pattern's rule is to _____ and then _____.

10,813, 3,604, 1,201, 400…

_____, _____

9) The pattern's rule is to _____ and then _____.

7,992, 3,896, 1,848, 824…

_____, _____

10) The pattern's rule is to _____ and then _____.

196,192, 49,248, 12,512, 3,328…

_____, _____

11) The pattern's rule is to _____ and then _____.

826, 410, 202, 98, 46…

_____, _____

12) The pattern's rule is to _____ and then _____.

1,159, 583, 295, 151, 79…

_____, _____

Shapes and Growing Number Patterns

Shapes can form growing patterns. The pattern grows in a predictable way, based on the pattern's rule. Figure out what the pattern's rule is, then use it to determine what comes next in the pattern.

Count the number of shapes in each term. They form a number pattern. Drawing the next set of shapes and counting them is one way to continue the number pattern, but drawing is not necessary once you recognize the number pattern's rule. The rule can be used to calculate the next numbers in the pattern without needing to draw more shapes.

Draw the next group of shapes in the pattern and write the number of shapes in this term.
Determine the number pattern's rule and use the rule to calculate the number of shapes for the next 2 terms of the pattern.

Example:

1   3   6

Answer:

1   3   6   10   15, 21...

Draw the next group of shapes in the pattern and write the number of shapes in this term.
Determine the number pattern's rule and use the rule to calculate the number of shapes for the next 2 terms of the pattern.

1) 1   4   9

2) 1   5   11

3) 1   5   9

4) 1   3   5

5) 3   5   7

6) 1   3   5

7) 1   4   7

8) 3   4   5

9) 1   3   6

10) 5   9   13

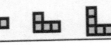
Draw the next group of shapes in the pattern and write the number of shapes in this term.
Determine the number pattern's rule and use the rule to calculate the number of shapes for the next 2 terms of the pattern.

1)   **1   4   7**

2)   **8   12   16**

3)   **1   4   9**

4)   **2   4   6**

5)   **2   5   8**

6)   **1   4   7**

7)   **4   6   8**

8)   **1   3   5**

9)   **1   6   11**

10)   **6   8   10**

11)   **5   10   15**

12)   **2   4   6**

13)   **4   7   10**

14)   **2   4   7**

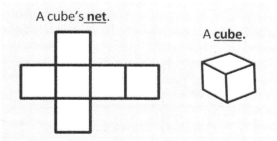

Nets and Cubes

If you take a 3-dimensional shape, such as a **cube**, open the sides, and lay them flat, they will create a **net**.

Today's problems will show a net of a cube. You'll need to imagine what the cube would look like if the net were to be folded into a cube. The pieces of the net are connected, so the sides of the cube cannot change locations.

A cube's **net**.

A **cube**.

Visualizing a net's cube.

Visualizing what a net will look like as a cube takes practice. Imagine how the sides will come together if the net were folded along the lines to form the edges of the cube. Focus on one square of the net. This will become one face on the cube. *What other faces on the cube will be next to the original face you were focusing on? Which face is on the opposite side of the cube from the face you had been focusing on?*

Imagine that the net is folded into a cube. Three of the images are examples of what that cube would look like from different angles. One of the four images is not an example of what the cube would look like. Which cube cannot be created by this net? (Shade the letter A, B, C, or D to indicate your answer.)

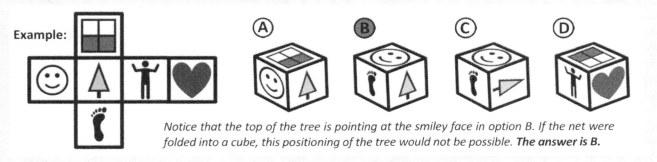

Example:

Ⓐ Ⓑ Ⓒ Ⓓ

*Notice that the top of the tree is pointing at the smiley face in option B. If the net were folded into a cube, this positioning of the tree would not be possible. **The answer is B.***

Imagine that the net is folded into a cube. Three of the images are examples of what that cube would look like from different angles. One of the four images is not an example of what the cube would look like. Which cube cannot be created by this net? (Shade the letter A, B, C, or D to indicate your answer.)

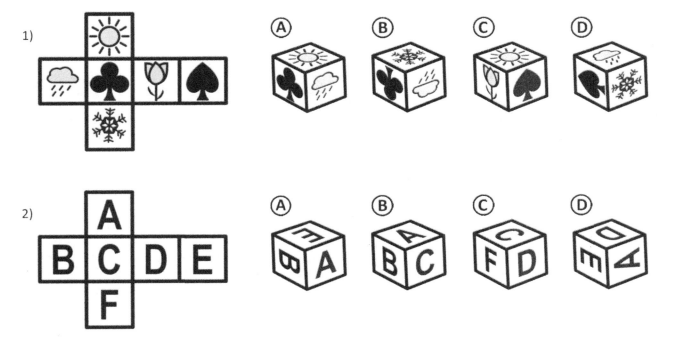

1)

Ⓐ Ⓑ Ⓒ Ⓓ

2)

Ⓐ Ⓑ Ⓒ Ⓓ

Name: _____

Score:

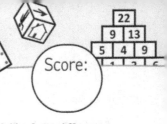

*Imagine that the net is folded into a cube. Three of the images are examples of what that cube would look like from different angles. One of the four images is **not** an example of what the cube would look like. Which cube cannot be created by this net? (Shade the letter A, B, C, or D to indicate your answer.)*

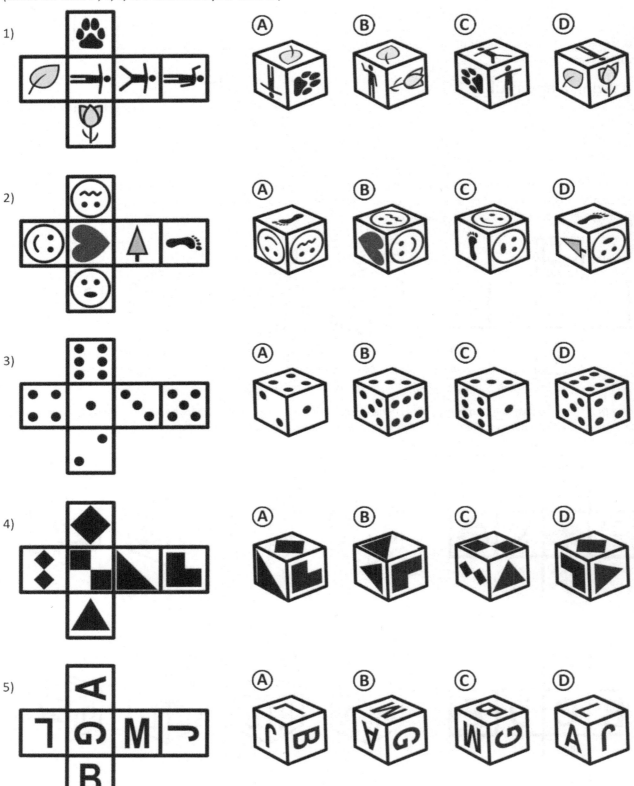

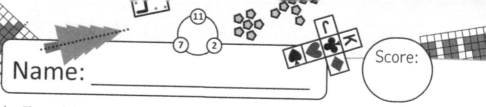

Name: _____

Score:

Imagine that the net is folded into a cube. Three of the images are examples of what that cube would look like from different angles. One of the four images is <u>not</u> an example of what the cube would look like. Which cube cannot be created by this net? (Shade the letter A, B, C, or D to indicate your answer.)

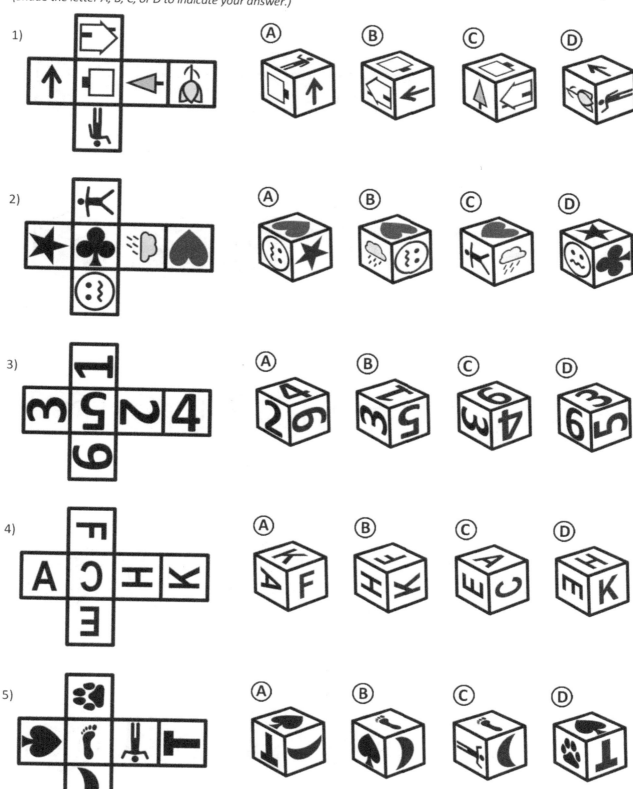

Puzzle

Imagine that the net is folded into a cube. Three of the images are examples of what that cube would look like from different angles. One of the four images is _not_ an example of what the cube would look like. Which cube cannot be created by this net? (Shade the letter A, B, C, or D to indicate your answer.)

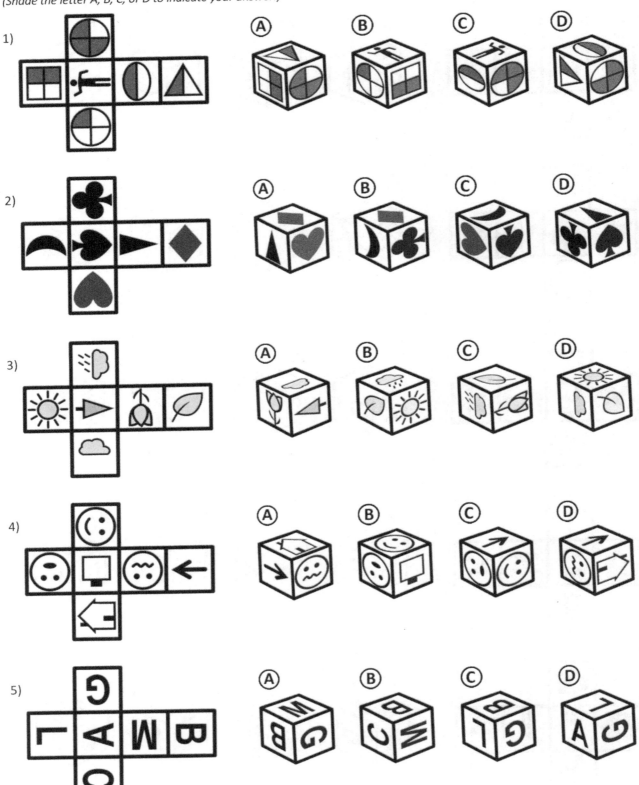

1)   A   B   C   D

2)   A   B   C   D

3)   A   B   C   D

4)   A   B   C   D

5)   A   B   C   D

Name: _____

Score:

A Missing Cube Face

Instead of determining which cube cannot be created by a net, today's goal will be for you to determine what the face of a cube will look like after viewing the net of the cube. You will need to determine what image needs to be on the cube's face and what direction that image needs to be rotated.

Drawing the Missing Cube Face

You must draw each missing cube face. Your drawings do not need to be perfect. Do your best. Focus on identifying which image needs to be drawn and which direction that image should be rotated. To do this, look at the cube faces that are known. Imagine the net when it's folded into a cube. *What image will be next to the known cube faces?*

Imagine that the net is folded into a cube. The images to the right are examples of what that cube would look like from different angles, except one cube face is blank. Based on the positioning of the known faces, draw the image on the face that is missing.

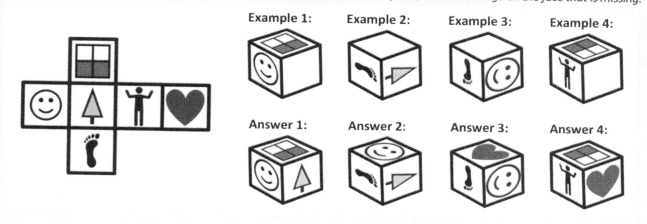

Imagine that the net is folded into a cube. The images to the right are examples of what that cube would look like from different angles, except one cube face is blank. Based on the positioning of the known faces, draw the image on the face that is missing. ✂ (*You may cut out the net and fold it into a cube to check your answer.*)

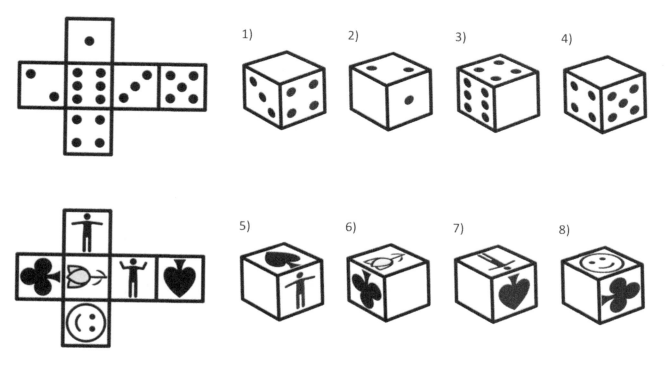

Name: _____

Score:

Imagine that the net is folded into a cube. The images to the right are examples of what that cube would look like from different angles, except one cube face is blank. Based on the positioning of the known faces, draw the image on the face that is missing. (You may cut out the net and fold it into a cube <u>to check your answer</u>.)

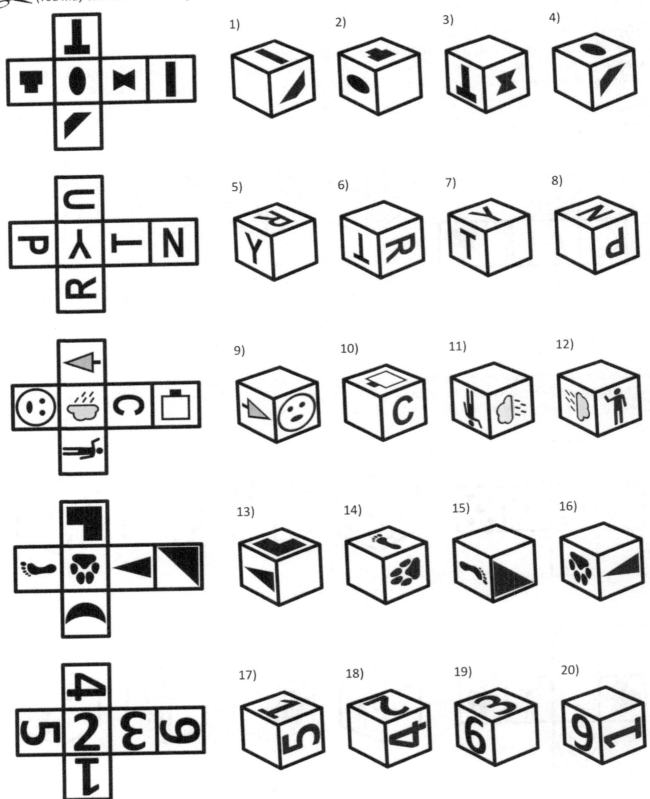

1)

2)

3)

4)

5)

6)

7)

8)

9)

10)

11)

12)

13)

14)

15)

16)

17)

18)

19)

20)

Name: _____

Score:

Imagine that the net is folded into a cube. The images to the right are examples of what that cube would look like from different angles, except one cube face is blank. Based on the positioning of the known faces, draw the image on the face that is missing. (You may cut out the net and fold it into a cube to check your answer.)

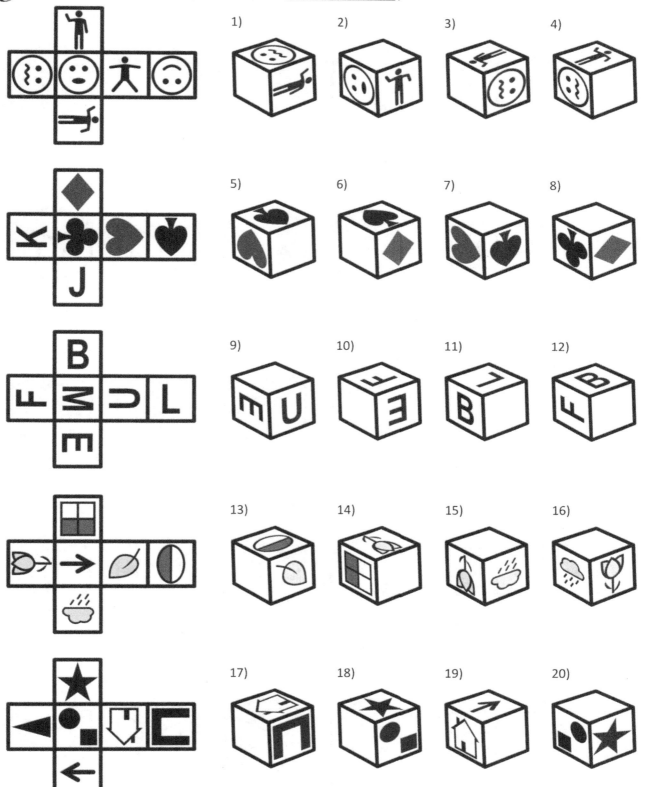

1)

2)

3)

4)

5)

6)

7)

8)

9)

10)

11)

12)

13)

14)

15)

16)

17)

18)

19)

20)

Day 79
Visual Spatial Cubes

Name: _____

Score:

Imagine that the net is folded into a cube. The images to the right are examples of what that cube would look like from different angles, except one cube face is blank. Based on the positioning of the known faces, draw the image on the face that is missing. (You may cut out the net and fold it into a cube to check your answer.)

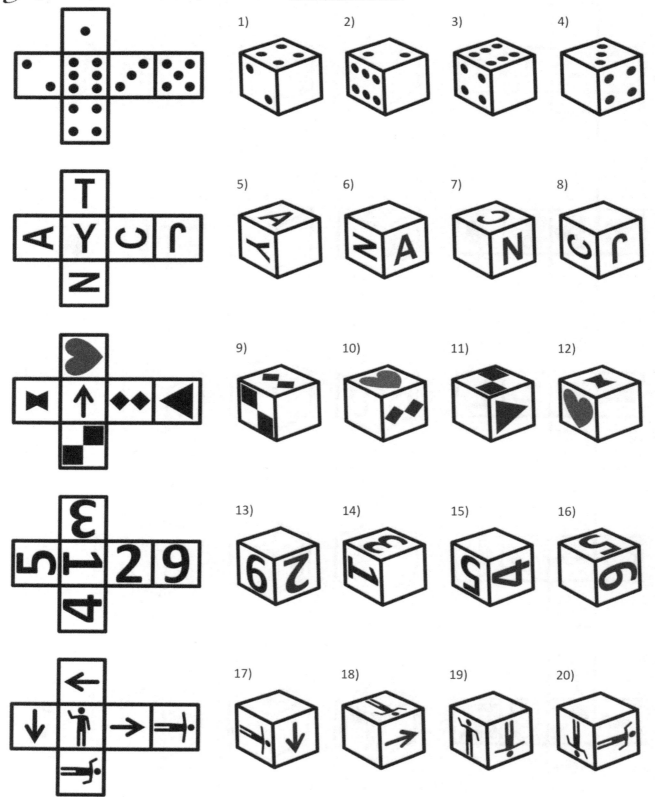

1) 2) 3) 4)

5) 6) 7) 8)

9) 10) 11) 12)

13) 14) 15) 16)

17) 18) 19) 20)

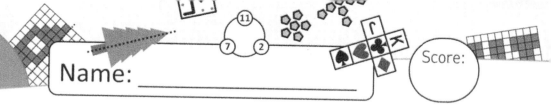

Different Style Nets

So far, the nets have looked similar to a lower-case t, but this is just one way to draw the net of a cube. They can be drawn many ways. Despite their different arrangements, each of the nets in this section can be folded into a cube.

Imagining the Cube

It can be difficult to imagine the entire net folded as a cube. In the problems below, you only need to visualize three of the cube faces, and two of them are already drawn for you. Imagine how the net would fold by these two known cube faces. What image is next two these two faces on the net? How would that image be orientated when it's folded too?

Imagine that the net is folded into a cube. The images to the right are examples of what that cube would look like from different angles, except one cube face is blank. Based on the positioning of the known faces, draw the image on the face that is missing.

Imagine that the net is folded into a cube. The images to the right are examples of what that cube would look like from different angles, except one cube face is blank. Based on the positioning of the known faces, draw the image on the face that is missing.

✂ (*You may cut out the net and fold it into a cube to check your answer.*)

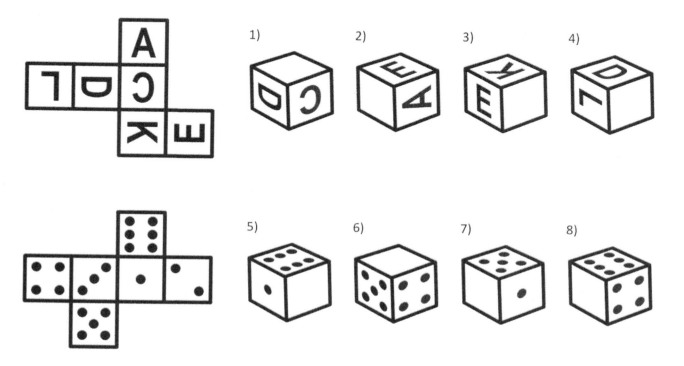

Puzzle

Name: _____

Score:

Imagine that the net is folded into a cube. The images to the right are examples of what that cube would look like from different angles, except one cube face is blank. Based on the positioning of the known faces, draw the image on the face that is missing. (You may cut out the net and fold it into a cube **to check your answer**.)

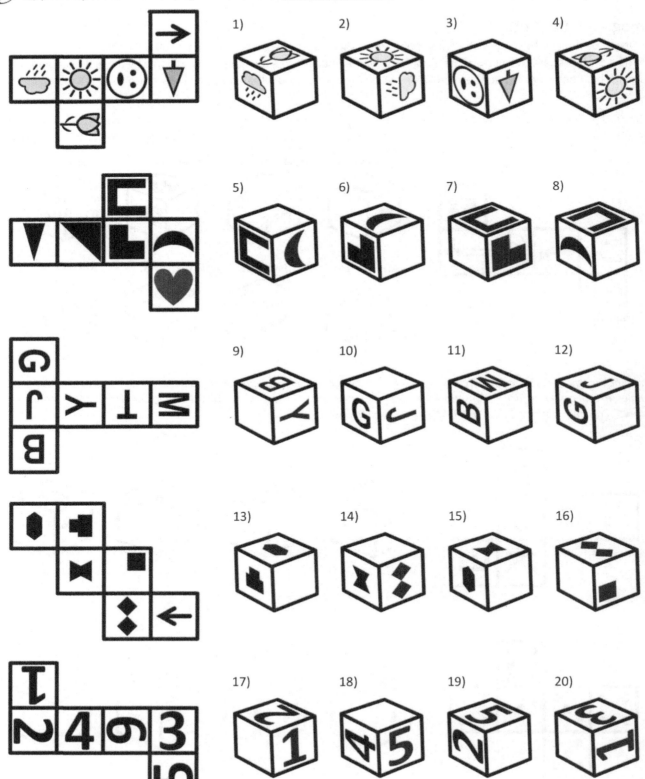

1) 2) 3) 4)

5) 6) 7) 8)

9) 10) 11) 12)

13) 14) 15) 16)

17) 18) 19) 20)

Name: _____

Score:

Imagine that the net is folded into a cube. The images to the right are examples of what that cube would look like from different angles, except one cube face is blank. Based on the positioning of the known faces, draw the image on the face that is missing. (You may cut out the net and fold it into a cube *to check your answer*.)

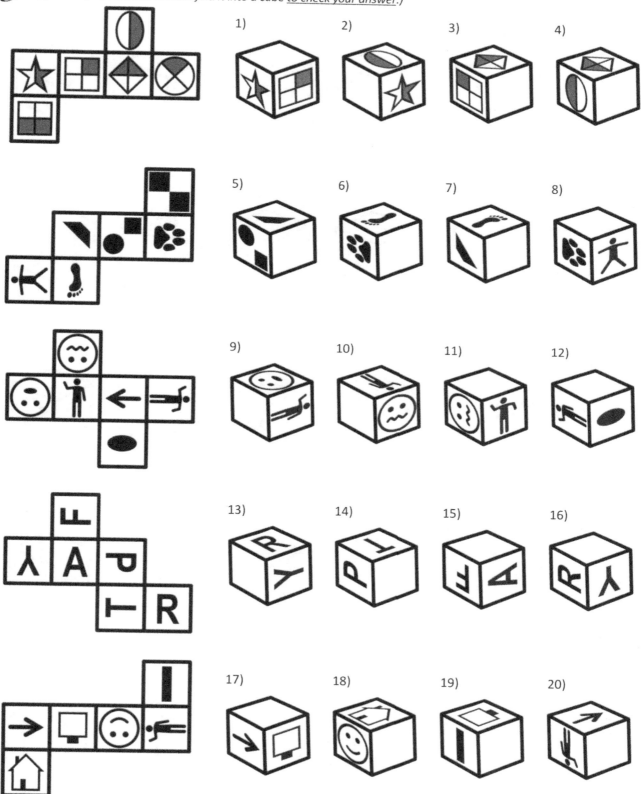

1)

2)

3)

4)

5)

6)

7)

8)

9)

10)

11)

12)

13)

14)

15)

16)

17)

18)

19)

20)

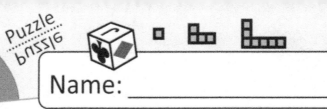

Puzzle

Name: _____

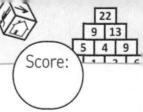

Score:

Imagine that the net is folded into a cube. The images to the right are examples of what that cube would look like from different angles, except one cube face is blank. Based on the positioning of the known faces, draw the image on the face that is missing. ✂ (You may cut out the net and fold it into a cube _to check your answer._)

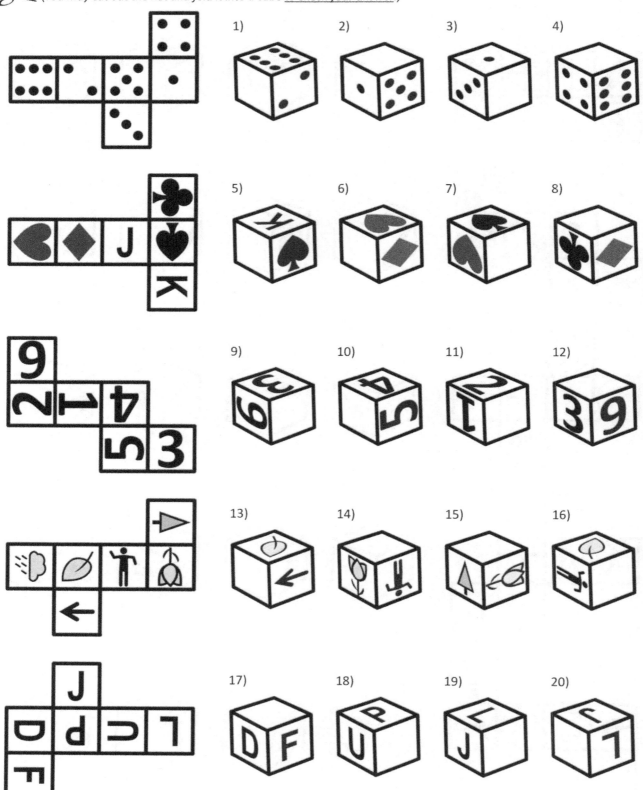

1)

2)

3)

4)

5)

6)

7)

8)

9)

10)

11)

12)

13)

14)

15)

16)

17)

18)

19)

20)

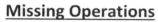

Name: _____

Score:

Missing Operations

Today, you will be given incomplete number sentences. The operations for these sentences are missing. You will need to figure out what operations are needed to make each number sentence true.

The operations to choose from are addition, subtraction, multiplication, and division. Any combination of these operations may be used. The operations may be different, such as multiplication and addition, or the same operation, such as subtraction and subtraction.

Write the missing operations that will make the number sentence true.

Example:

$$5 \bigcirc 4 \bigcirc 8 = 28$$

Answer:

$$5 \otimes 4 \oplus 8 = 28$$

The **order of operations** (**PEMDAS** or **BODMAS**) <u>are not used</u> in the number sentences for the problems in this book. *Since this skill has not been taught yet, please perform all operations from left to right. **If using a calculator**, operations may need to be entered and calculated **one at a time**, from left to right to get the same answers as the answer key.*

Write the missing operations that will make each number sentence true. (*Perform all operations from left to right.*)

1) $5 \bigcirc 6 \bigcirc 10 = 3$

2) $200 \bigcirc 50 \bigcirc 3 = 450$

3) $100 \bigcirc 2 \bigcirc 10 = 40$

4) $4 \bigcirc 7 \bigcirc 4 = 44$

5) $10 \bigcirc 4 \bigcirc 3 = 120$

6) $35 \bigcirc 20 \bigcirc 3 = 5$

7) $5 \bigcirc 10 \bigcirc 12 = 27$

8) $30 \bigcirc 5 \bigcirc 4 = 100$

9) $100 \bigcirc 5 \bigcirc 4 = 80$

10) $50 \bigcirc 4 \bigcirc 3 = 600$

11) $60 \bigcirc 5 \bigcirc 3 = 9$

12) $80 \bigcirc 20 \bigcirc 10 = 110$

13) $500 \bigcirc 2 \bigcirc 10 = 100$

14) $8 \bigcirc 4 \bigcirc 6 = 26$

15) $20 \bigcirc 5 \bigcirc 7 = 28$

16) $7 \bigcirc 5 \bigcirc 15 = 30$

17) $50 \bigcirc 20 \bigcirc 4 = 26$

18) $60 \bigcirc 15 \bigcirc 9 = 5$

19) $4 \bigcirc 3 \bigcirc 3 = 15$

20) $10 \bigcirc 10 \bigcirc 5 = 6$

21) $8 \bigcirc 6 \bigcirc 1 = 3$

22) $10 \bigcirc 5 \bigcirc 5 = 25$

23) $10 \bigcirc 5 \bigcirc 5 = 7$

24) $10 \bigcirc 5 \bigcirc 5 = 55$

25) $10 \bigcirc 5 \bigcirc 5 = 250$

26) $10 \bigcirc 5 \bigcirc 5 = 45$

Write the missing operations that will make each number sentence true.
*(The **order of operations** are not used in this book. Perform all operations from left to right.)*

1) $9 \bigcirc 3 \bigcirc 3 = 6$

2) $9 \bigcirc 3 \bigcirc 3 = 30$

3) $9 \bigcirc 3 \bigcirc 3 = 3$

4) $9 \bigcirc 3 \bigcirc 3 = 1$

5) $100 \bigcirc 4 \bigcirc 10 = 40$

6) $100 \bigcirc 4 \bigcirc 10 = 250$

7) $100 \bigcirc 4 \bigcirc 10 = 35$

8) $100 \bigcirc 4 \bigcirc 10 = 960$

9) $100 \bigcirc 4 \bigcirc 10 = 390$

10) $24 \bigcirc 2 \bigcirc 5 = 43$

11) $24 \bigcirc 2 \bigcirc 5 = 60$

12) $24 \bigcirc 2 \bigcirc 5 = 110$

13) $40 \bigcirc 5 \bigcirc 3 = 15$

14) $40 \bigcirc 5 \bigcirc 3 = 5$

15) $40 \bigcirc 5 \bigcirc 3 = 105$

16) $12 \bigcirc 2 \bigcirc 10 = 140$

17) $12 \bigcirc 2 \bigcirc 10 = 240$

18) $12 \bigcirc 2 \bigcirc 10 = 16$

19) $12 \bigcirc 2 \bigcirc 10 = 100$

20) $20 \bigcirc 4 \bigcirc 2 = 40$

21) $20 \bigcirc 4 \bigcirc 2 = 10$

22) $20 \bigcirc 4 \bigcirc 2 = 12$

23) $20 \bigcirc 4 \bigcirc 2 = 3$

24) $60 \bigcirc 12 \bigcirc 5 = 25$

25) $60 \bigcirc 12 \bigcirc 5 = 53$

26) $200 \bigcirc 5 \bigcirc 10 = 100$

27) $200 \bigcirc 5 \bigcirc 10 = 4$

28) $200 \bigcirc 5 \bigcirc 10 = 185$

29) $200 \bigcirc 5 \bigcirc 10 = 10,000$

30) $200 \bigcirc 5 \bigcirc 10 = 1,950$

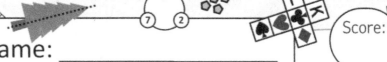

Name: _____

Score:

3 Missing Operations

Instead of 2 missing operations, today there will be 3 missing operations. This may not seem like a large change, but the extra operation makes solving these problems much more challenging. Hopefully you're ready for a challenge. Consider different ways you can use operations to solve each problem. Take your time. This is not a race.

The **order of operations** (*PEMDAS* or *BODMAS*) <u>are not used</u> in the number sentences for the problems in this book. Since this skill has not been taught yet, please perform all operations from left to right.

Write the missing operations that will make each number sentence true.
(The **order of operations** <u>are not used</u> in this book. Perform all operations from left to right.)

1) $5 \bigcirc 6 \bigcirc 2 \bigcirc 4 = 26$

2) $7 \bigcirc 3 \bigcirc 4 \bigcirc 10 = 7$

3) $3 \bigcirc 8 \bigcirc 20 \bigcirc 5 = 9$

4) $20 \bigcirc 4 \bigcirc 9 \bigcirc 40 = 5$

5) $2 \bigcirc 8 \bigcirc 5 \bigcirc 3 = 6$

6) $36 \bigcirc 6 \bigcirc 2 \bigcirc 7 = 10$

7) $14 \bigcirc 6 \bigcirc 2 \bigcirc 3 = 2$

8) $6 \bigcirc 1 \bigcirc 5 \bigcirc 10 = 25$

9) $9 \bigcirc 7 \bigcirc 6 \bigcirc 2 = 44$

10) $8 \bigcirc 5 \bigcirc 15 \bigcirc 5 = 5$

11) $80 \bigcirc 40 \bigcirc 20 \bigcirc 7 = 27$

12) $18 \bigcirc 6 \bigcirc 8 \bigcirc 2 = 9$

13) $1 \bigcirc 1 \bigcirc 3 \bigcirc 4 = 20$

14) $24 \bigcirc 4 \bigcirc 3 \bigcirc 7 = 14$

15) $4 \bigcirc 7 \bigcirc 6 \bigcirc 2 = 11$

16) $90 \bigcirc 10 \bigcirc 3 \bigcirc 17 = 20$

17) $4 \bigcirc 3 \bigcirc 1 \bigcirc 7 = 4$

18) $5 \bigcirc 4 \bigcirc 2 \bigcirc 8 = 2$

19) $3 \bigcirc 6 \bigcirc 2 \bigcirc 5 = 12$

20) $100 \bigcirc 20 \bigcirc 9 \bigcirc 5 = 50$

21) $50 \bigcirc 20 \bigcirc 10 \bigcirc 3 = 120$

22) $2 \bigcirc 3 \bigcirc 4 \bigcirc 12 = 120$

23) $8 \bigcirc 4 \bigcirc 7 \bigcirc 3 = 3$

24) $9 \bigcirc 6 \bigcirc 5 \bigcirc 8 = 80$

25) $60 \bigcirc 30 \bigcirc 10 \bigcirc 2 = 5$

26) $1 \bigcirc 2 \bigcirc 4 \bigcirc 6 = 36$

Puzzle

Name: _____

Score:

Write the missing operations that will make each number sentence true.
*(The **order of operations** are not used in this book. Perform all operations from left to right.)*

1) 8 ◯ 2 ◯ 5 ◯ 3 = 15

2) 120 ◯ 10 ◯ 3 ◯ 6 = 9

3) 4 ◯ 7 ◯ 28 ◯ 3 = 4

4) 9 ◯ 5 ◯ 3 ◯ 2 = 6

5) 100 ◯ 4 ◯ 2 ◯ 25 = 25

6) 4 ◯ 5 ◯ 4 ◯ 6 = 22

7) 10 ◯ 3 ◯ 9 ◯ 16 = 1

8) 9 ◯ 4 ◯ 3 ◯ 5 = 11

9) 6 ◯ 2 ◯ 2 ◯ 8 = 3

10) 7 ◯ 4 ◯ 2 ◯ 200 = 200

11) 50 ◯ 10 ◯ 5 ◯ 40 = 41

12) 3 ◯ 7 ◯ 8 ◯ 9 = 18

13) 15 ◯ 5 ◯ 20 ◯ 40 = 160

14) 6 ◯ 7 ◯ 42 ◯ 6 = 7

15) 24 ◯ 2 ◯ 8 ◯ 5 = 15

16) 9 ◯ 2 ◯ 12 ◯ 4 = 10

17) 70 ◯ 30 ◯ 60 ◯ 4 = 40

18) 11 ◯ 6 ◯ 4 ◯ 1 = 19

19) 2 ◯ 4 ◯ 8 ◯ 99 = 100

20) 30 ◯ 3 ◯ 13 ◯ 5 = 28

21) 4 ◯ 10 ◯ 2 ◯ 30 = 110

22) 6 ◯ 2 ◯ 12 ◯ 5 = 3

23) 81 ◯ 9 ◯ 1 ◯ 2 = 5

24) 3 ◯ 9 ◯ 10 ◯ 20 = 140

25) 75 ◯ 70 ◯ 5 ◯ 5 = 50

26) 3 ◯ 7 ◯ 7 ◯ 2 = 14

27) 9 ◯ 5 ◯ 15 ◯ 10 = 3

28) 5 ◯ 9 ◯ 2 ◯ 4 = 32

29) 7 ◯ 5 ◯ 1 ◯ 4 = 38

30) 9 ◯ 5 ◯ 6 ◯ 8 = 3

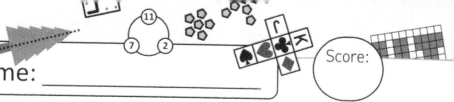

Day 88

3 Missing Operations

Name: _____

Score: _____

Write the missing operations that will make each number sentence true.
*(The **order of operations** are not used in this book. Perform all operations from left to right.)*

1) 60 ◯ 30 ◯ 5 ◯ 4 = 40

2) 11 ◯ 6 ◯ 8 ◯ 1 = 41

3) 5 ◯ 8 ◯ 3 ◯ 5 = 125

4) 9 ◯ 3 ◯ 20 ◯ 7 = 1

5) 7 ◯ 4 ◯ 3 ◯ 2 = 50

6) 4 ◯ 5 ◯ 4 ◯ 6 = 22

7) 18 ◯ 2 ◯ 7 ◯ 1 = 1

8) 5 ◯ 4 ◯ 3 ◯ 8 = 12

9) 8 ◯ 5 ◯ 4 ◯ 2 = 10

10) 2 ◯ 6 ◯ 5 ◯ 7 = 6

11) 87 ◯ 7 ◯ 8 ◯ 2 = 20

12) 2 ◯ 25 ◯ 2 ◯ 6 = 8

13) 7 ◯ 5 ◯ 5 ◯ 1 = 39

14) 8 ◯ 8 ◯ 6 ◯ 4 = 28

15) 10 ◯ 7 ◯ 8 ◯ 2 = 12

16) 1 ◯ 9 ◯ 2 ◯ 8 = 3

17) 2 ◯ 4 ◯ 6 ◯ 3 = 108

18) 62 ◯ 7 ◯ 5 ◯ 1 = 12

19) 3 ◯ 6 ◯ 9 ◯ 200 = 227

20) 500 ◯ 4 ◯ 3 ◯ 2 = 120

21) 29 ◯ 9 ◯ 6 ◯ 4 = 8

22) 45 ◯ 15 ◯ 30 ◯ 9 = 24

23) 8 ◯ 4 ◯ 12 ◯ 7 = 27

24) 16 ◯ 6 ◯ 3 ◯ 5 = 6

25) 7 ◯ 5 ◯ 6 ◯ 2 = 31

26) 60 ◯ 20 ◯ 4 ◯ 5 = 17

27) 90 ◯ 70 ◯ 40 ◯ 11 = 44

28) 8 ◯ 5 ◯ 6 ◯ 90 = 150

29) 3 ◯ 1 ◯ 6 ◯ 4 = 32

30) 250 ◯ 50 ◯ 50 ◯ 7 = 50

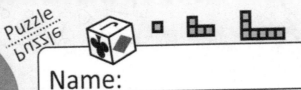

Puzzle

Name: _____

Score:

Write the missing operations that will make each number sentence true.
(The **order of operations** <u>are not used</u> in this book. Perform all operations from left to right.)

1) $1{,}000 \bigcirc 20 \bigcirc 10 \bigcirc 5 = 55$

2) $7 \bigcirc 5 \bigcirc 2 \bigcirc 3 = 73$

3) $96 \bigcirc 6 \bigcirc 40 \bigcirc 13 = 10$

4) $8 \bigcirc 1 \bigcirc 3 \bigcirc 5 = 30$

5) $4 \bigcirc 9 \bigcirc 7 \bigcirc 6 = 23$

6) $25 \bigcirc 5 \bigcirc 9 \bigcirc 1 = 15$

7) $6 \bigcirc 3 \bigcirc 3 \bigcirc 4 = 48$

8) $900 \bigcirc 600 \bigcirc 50 \bigcirc 250 = 1$

9) $36 \bigcirc 24 \bigcirc 15 \bigcirc 2 = 6$

10) $88 \bigcirc 80 \bigcirc 4 \bigcirc 6 = 38$

11) $5 \bigcirc 15 \bigcirc 4 \bigcirc 8 = 40$

12) $9 \bigcirc 3 \bigcirc 5 \bigcirc 3 = 90$

13) $4 \bigcirc 6 \bigcirc 6 \bigcirc 3 = 10$

14) $70 \bigcirc 20 \bigcirc 3 \bigcirc 70 = 200$

15) $120 \bigcirc 50 \bigcirc 70 \bigcirc 16 = 17$

16) $144 \bigcirc 12 \bigcirc 3 \bigcirc 5 = 75$

17) $2 \bigcirc 20 \bigcirc 10 \bigcirc 2 = 60$

18) $700 \bigcirc 300 \bigcirc 50 \bigcirc 4 = 4$

19) $39 \bigcirc 1 \bigcirc 12 \bigcirc 20 = 500$

20) $16 \bigcirc 4 \bigcirc 24 \bigcirc 2 = 14$

21) $19 \bigcirc 17 \bigcirc 8 \bigcirc 4 = 11$

22) $24 \bigcirc 4 \bigcirc 16 \bigcirc 20 = 100$

23) $80 \bigcirc 5 \bigcirc 3 \bigcirc 9 = 57$

24) $5 \bigcirc 6 \bigcirc 7 \bigcirc 8 = 12$

25) $24 \bigcirc 4 \bigcirc 3 \bigcirc 9 = 11$

26) $98 \bigcirc 7 \bigcirc 90 \bigcirc 4 = 60$

27) $6 \bigcirc 1 \bigcirc 10 \bigcirc 3 = 5$

28) $9 \bigcirc 4 \bigcirc 8 \bigcirc 5 = 25$

29) $1 \bigcirc 9 \bigcirc 5 \bigcirc 5 = 50$

30) $8 \bigcirc 6 \bigcirc 7 \bigcirc 8 = 90$

Name: _____

Score:

4 Missing Operations

Would you agree that finding 3 missing operations was more difficult than 2? Well, here's your chance to find 4 missing operations. Expect these problems to be more challenging and take more time. They may be difficult, but far from impossible. With enough determination, you should be able to solve each one.

Write the missing operations that will make each number sentence true.
*(The **order of operations** are not used in this book. Perform all operations from left to right.)*

1) $15 \bigcirc 3 \bigcirc 7 \bigcirc 10 \bigcirc 1 = 24$

2) $9 \bigcirc 6 \bigcirc 3 \bigcirc 1 \bigcirc 23 = 2$

3) $7 \bigcirc 5 \bigcirc 10 \bigcirc 2 \bigcirc 5 = 8$

4) $6 \bigcirc 5 \bigcirc 4 \bigcirc 3 \bigcirc 10 = 30$

5) $4 \bigcirc 4 \bigcirc 5 \bigcirc 17 \bigcirc 9 = 37$

6) $30 \bigcirc 2 \bigcirc 5 \bigcirc 4 \bigcirc 2 = 3$

7) $1 \bigcirc 76 \bigcirc 11 \bigcirc 3 \bigcirc 8 = 32$

8) $2 \bigcirc 1 \bigcirc 66 \bigcirc 34 \bigcirc 20 = 5$

9) $8 \bigcirc 5 \bigcirc 4 \bigcirc 7 \bigcirc 4 = 7$

10) $3 \bigcirc 11 \bigcirc 7 \bigcirc 7 \bigcirc 71 = 71$

11) $99 \bigcirc 9 \bigcirc 4 \bigcirc 35 \bigcirc 10 = 5$

12) $7 \bigcirc 2 \bigcirc 3 \bigcirc 4 \bigcirc 7 = 37$

13) $8 \bigcirc 5 \bigcirc 7 \bigcirc 10 \bigcirc 15 = 30$

14) $16 \bigcirc 4 \bigcirc 5 \bigcirc 6 \bigcirc 8 = 22$

15) $4 \bigcirc 2 \bigcirc 72 \bigcirc 50 \bigcirc 3 = 90$

16) $6 \bigcirc 7 \bigcirc 7 \bigcirc 4 \bigcirc 2 = 18$

17) $57 \bigcirc 6 \bigcirc 18 \bigcirc 4 \bigcirc 5 = 185$

18) $9 \bigcirc 31 \bigcirc 2 \bigcirc 8 \bigcirc 4 = 7$

19) $14 \bigcirc 7 \bigcirc 8 \bigcirc 6 \bigcirc 9 = 36$

20) $2 \bigcirc 5 \bigcirc 4 \bigcirc 3 \bigcirc 66 = 68$

21) $48 \bigcirc 16 \bigcirc 8 \bigcirc 1 \bigcirc 6 = 11$

22) $3 \bigcirc 51 \bigcirc 9 \bigcirc 13 \bigcirc 2 = 25$

23) $7 \bigcirc 6 \bigcirc 8 \bigcirc 2 \bigcirc 13 = 12$

24) $9 \bigcirc 6 \bigcirc 10 \bigcirc 70 \bigcirc 30 = 110$

25) $1 \bigcirc 50 \bigcirc 20 \bigcirc 16 \bigcirc 14 = 40$

26) $36 \bigcirc 6 \bigcirc 8 \bigcirc 12 \bigcirc 9 = 27$

Operation Circles

Operation circles have numbers around the outside of the circle. <u>Between the numbers are unknown operations</u>. These numbers and operations form a number sentence that is equal to the number in the center of the circle. <u>You need to figure out where the number sentence begins</u>, and <u>what operations are used</u> in the number sentence.

- **All the numbers** on the outside of the circle need to be used in the number sentence.
- After beginning with the first number, the numbers in the number sentence must follow the perimeter of the circle **clockwise or counterclockwise**, using the numbers in the order that they appear on the circle.
- Ask yourself "**what operations** could be placed between the numbers on the number circle to form a number sentence that will equal the number in the center of the circle."
- It may help to **write the operations** around the outside of the circle.
- Due to the commutative property of addition and multiplication, some operation circles may have more than one number sentence. (Example 1 below may be $4 \times 5 - 2 = 18$ or $5 \times 4 - 2 = 18$.)

Write a number sentence for each operation circle.

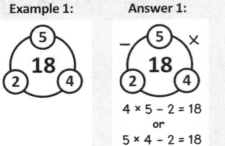

Example 1: **Answer 1:**

$4 \times 5 - 2 = 18$
or
$5 \times 4 - 2 = 18$

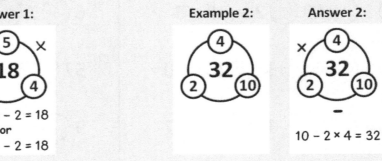

Example 2: **Answer 2:**

$10 - 2 \times 4 = 32$

The **order of operations (PEMDAS** or **BODMAS)** <u>are not used</u> in the number sentences for the problems in this book. Since this skill has not been taught yet, operations in number sentences will be written and performed from left to right.

*Write a number sentence for each operation circle. (The **order of operations** are not used in this book.)*

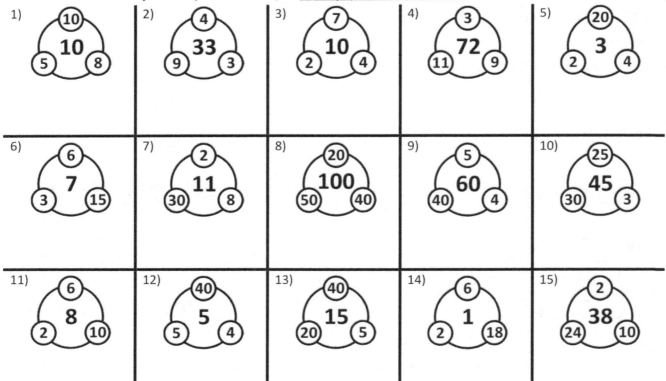

Name: _____

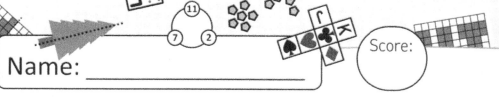

Operation Circle Puzzles

Operation circle puzzles involve multiple operation circles. All the operation circles in the puzzle will use the same operations, in the same locations, and in the same order. The challenge is that one of the operation circles will have an unknown number. You need to calculate the unknown number based on the information available.

Write a number sentence to calculate the unknown number.

Example:

Answer:

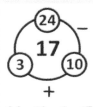

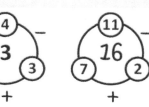

24 – 10 + 3 = 17   4 – 3 + 2 = 3   11 – 2 + 7 = 16

Notice how the same operations are used in the same order. The number sentences for each operation circle are also written, but <u>this is not required</u>. Writing each number sentence may help you visualize the operations and their sequence, but <u>only the number sentence for the operation circle with the missing number is needed</u>.

*Write a number sentence to calculate the unknown number. (The **order of operations** are not used in this book.)*

1)

2)

3)

4)

5)

6)

7)

8)

  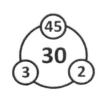 

Day 93
Operation Circles

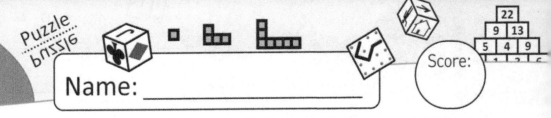

Name: _____

Score: _____

Calculate the unknown number and write the number sentence for its operation circle. (*The **order of operations** are not used.*)

1)

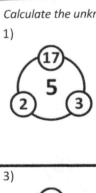 top 17, center 5, bottom-left 2, bottom-right 3

 top 20, center 7, bottom-left 6, bottom-right 2

 top 25, bottom-left 7, bottom-right 3

2)

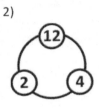 top 12, bottom-left 2, bottom-right 4

 top 48, center 30, bottom-left 6, bottom-right 2

 top 6, center 10, bottom-left 8, bottom-right 3

3)

 top 5, center 15, bottom-left 4, bottom-right 1

 top 7, bottom-left 13, bottom-right 9

 top 4, center 8, bottom-left 10, bottom-right 8

4)

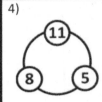 top 11, bottom-left 8, bottom-right 5

 top 12, center 9, bottom-left 4, bottom-right 24

 top 12, center 8, bottom-left 2, bottom-right 4

5)

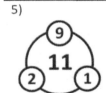 top 9, center 11, bottom-left 2, bottom-right 1

 top 6, center 14, bottom-left 1, bottom-right 8

 top 5, bottom-left 4, bottom-right 2

6)

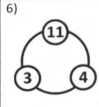 top 11, bottom-left 3, bottom-right 4

 top 6, center 28, bottom-left 2, bottom-right 8

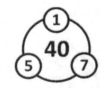 top 1, center 40, bottom-left 5, bottom-right 7

7)

 top 22, center 32, bottom-left 6, bottom-right 2

 top 5, bottom-left 1, bottom-right 6

 top 9, center 21, bottom-left 6, bottom-right 7

8)

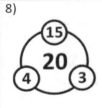 top 15, center 20, bottom-left 4, bottom-right 3

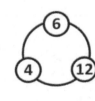 top 6, bottom-left 4, bottom-right 12

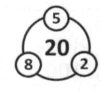 top 5, center 20, bottom-left 8, bottom-right 2

9)

 top 11, center 13, bottom-left 3, bottom-right 6

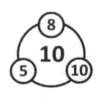 top 8, center 10, bottom-left 5, bottom-right 10

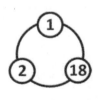 top 1, bottom-left 2, bottom-right 18

10)

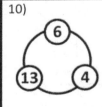 top 6, bottom-left 13, bottom-right 4

 top 7, center 15, bottom-left 3, bottom-right 2

 top 11, center 20, bottom-left 4, bottom-right 6

11)

 top 8, center 10, bottom-left 5, bottom-right 4

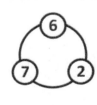 top 6, bottom-left 7, bottom-right 2

 top 12, center 18, bottom-left 3, bottom-right 2

12)

 top 9, center 3, bottom-left 6, bottom-right 2

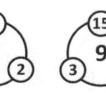 top 15, center 9, bottom-left 3, bottom-right 8

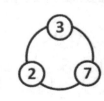 top 3, bottom-left 2, bottom-right 7

Name: _____

Score:

Sudoku

Sudoku is a popular number puzzle and that is not hard to learn. Sudoku uses a 9 by 9 grid. Only some of the numbers in the grid are known. You need to figure out the rest of the numbers. There are some strategies that can be used to find the missing numbers using the rules to the right.

Sudoku Rules:
- Only numbers *1 through 9* are used.
- Each **row** cannot repeat a number.
- Each **column** cannot repeat a number
- Each 3x3 **square** cannot repeat a number.

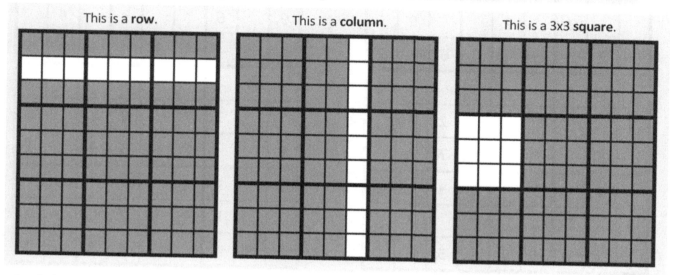

This is a **row**.   This is a **column**.   This is a 3x3 **square**.

Sudoku Strategies

Do any of the rows, columns, or 3x3 squares, have 8 known numbers? If so, which number 1 through 9 has not been used yet. That's the missing number.

Do any columns have 7 known numbers? If so, only two numbers haven't been used yet. Look at the rows and squares that pass through the column. Have either of the unused numbers already been used in these rows or squares?

The best strategy for learning sudoku is **finding a friend** that knows how to solve these puzzles and ask them to teach you their strategies. Solve some of these puzzles with them and have them explain their steps and thought processes.

Find the unknown numbers for each sudoku puzzle.

1)

7	6	9			3	1	2	5
8	2			1	5	4		9
4		5	6	2	9		8	
6		4	3	5			7	8
	8	1	2		6	9		4
2			9	8		6	3	1
5	3			1		2	7	4
	4	2	5	6	7	8		3
	7	6	4	3	8		1	2

2)

	1	2	7	6	5	3		
5		3					2	1
7	4		1	2	3	9	6	5
8	3		6	1	2	5		7
1	5	6		4		2		8
	7	4	3		8	6		9
4			2	3			7	
6	2	7	5		1	4	9	3
3			4	7	6		5	

Day 95
Sudoku Puzzles

Puzzle

Name: _____

Score:

Find the unknown numbers for each sudoku puzzle.

1)

4	9	7	6		3	8		
		3		2			9	5
	2		8	4		6		7
	4	6	2		5		8	3
3		9		4	2	5		
	5		9		8	7		
	1		5		6	3		9
6	7	5					4	
	3		4	7	1	5		6

2)

	8	7		6	9			2
9		6			3		4	
	2		8	7		6	9	5
5	6			3	2		8	7
		3	7		8			6
8			6	9	5	3		1
1		2	4		7		6	
7			8	9	5			3
6	9				1	8		4

3)

9		7		4	3	6		5
1	3			2	7	4		
5			9	7			3	
6		3						4
	9	2		6		3	5	1
4	5			3		2		
	4	5		2		9		3
	6		8		4			7
2		9	3	1		4		8

4)

	7		8					9
4		3			2	5	7	6
6			4	5				
2			9					3
	4		2	8		9		
1		9		3		2		5
9		5	6		8		2	7
	2					1		4
		4	5		1			

Name: _____

Score:

Find the unknown numbers for each sudoku puzzle.

1)

	5	9	1	8			4	
8	2		5		4	3		9
3		4				5		1
4		2		5	8	1	6	7
6		8						4
1	9		4	7			3	
2			6	4		7	9	
	1		8		5			6
5		6		9				3

2)

	1	5	8		7			4
4		7	3			9		2
	2			9	4		7	
	3	1		4		6	9	8
7	4		6		9			5
2		9	1	5		4	3	
6				8		1		9
	5	4	9		1			
1				7	3	5		6

3)

1	2		5		4			7
8					3		4	1
		6	7	2		3		
			4					8
6	9	8		1		5	3	
		4	8		9		7	
		9			5	7		
4	5			6			1	
2				7	8	4		9

4)

4	5		3		9	7	6	
8	9				7	5		4
1			4				3	
	8	9	7		1	4	5	2
6			5					3
	4	5	9		8	1	7	6
7		1		5		3	8	
	2	4	8					7
9	3			7	6	2		5

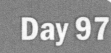

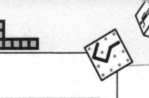
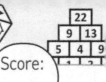

Name: _____

Score:

Cross-Number Puzzles

A cross-number puzzle is like a crossword puzzle, except it uses number sentences instead of words. You need to figure out what number belongs in each blank box to make the number sentences true. Since the rows and columns cross one another, the number in each box will be used in two different number sentences—one for the column and one for the row.

Example:

15	−		=	
+		+		+
	−		=	11
=		=		=
27	−		=	19

Answer:

15	−	7	=	8
+		+		+
12	−	1	=	11
=		=		=
27	−	8	=	19

Inverse Operations

Inverse operations may be used to calculate some of the unknown numbers. If a number sentence uses addition, subtraction may be used to find the missing number. For instance, the number sentence 15 + ? = 27 may be re-written as 27 − 15 = ?. Re-writing a number sentence may make it easier to calculate the missing number. In this example, 27 − 15 = 12. So, the missing number is 12.

Write a number in the blank boxes to make each number sentence true.

1)

	−	0	=	
+		+		+
	+		=	7
=		=		=
24	+		=	25

2)

17	+	24	=	
+		+		+
	+		=	36
=		=		=
	+	29	=	

3)

	+	12	=	
+		−		+
	−		=	3
=		=		=
31	+	0	=	

4)

45	−	28	=	
−		−		+
	+	2	=	
=		=		=
19	+		=	

5)

	−	19	=	10
+		+		+
	−		=	
=		=		=
48	−		=	18

6)

	+		=	72
+		−		+
68	−		=	
=		=		=
	+	3	=	83

7)

	+		=	67
−		+		−
38	−		=	10
=		=		=
	+	43	=	

8)

44	+		=	81
+		−		+
	−	24	=	
=		=		=
73	+		=	

9)

62	−		=	40
−		−		−
45	−		=	
=		=		=
	+		=	17

Name: _____

Score:

Longer Number Sentences

Cross-number puzzles can be different sizes. Some are made of short number sentences. Others involve longer number sentences. The same processes of using inverse operations may help to solve the puzzle.

Trial and Error

Many crossword puzzles are difficult to solve, yet crossword puzzles remain popular. People like the challenge of solving them. The same is true with cross-number puzzles. <u>They can be tricky to solve, but that's part of the **fun**.</u>

Solving a cross-number puzzle may require **trial and error**. <u>The problems in this book can be solved without this method. You should be able to systematically find a way to calculate each of the blank spaces in each puzzle.</u>

Cross-number puzzles you encounter in other places may not be designed this way. Sometimes, you may need to make logical guesses and see if they work to solve the puzzle. In such cases, it may be wise to lightly draw your guesses on the cross-number puzzle to see if they work. Only darken these numbers when you are confident that they are the correct ones.

Write a number in the blank boxes to make each number sentence true.

1)

28	−		+	14	=	
+		+		−		+
7	+		+		=	16
=		=		=		=
	+	9	+		=	51

2)

	−	75	+		−	13	=	5
+		−		+		+		+
19	+		−	6	+		=	68
=		=		=		=		=
99	−		−		+	33	=	

3)

	+	15	+		=	85
−		+		−		−
25	−		+	10	=	
=		=		=		=
20	+		+		=	70

4)

6	−		=	4
+		+		+
5	−	1	=	
−		+		+
	+	7	=	
=		=		=
	+		=	18

5)

18	−	7	=	
+		−		+
	−	2	=	
−		+		+
2	−		=	1
=		=		=
	−		=	16

6)

	−	8	+		=	30
+		−		+		+
10	+		−	6	=	
−		+		−		+
7	−	4	+		=	8
=		=		=		=
39	+	9	−	3	=	

7)

50	−	13	+	5	+		=	
+		+		+		+		+
	+	6	−		−		=	14
=		=		=		=		=
64	−		+	6	+	14	=	

© Libro Studio LLC 2024

More Operations

Time to mix it up a bit and include multiplication and division operations too. Remember that multiplication and division are inverse operations to one another, the same way addition and subtraction are inverse operations.

Write a number in the blank boxes to make each number sentence true.

1)

	÷	5	=	10
−		×		×
	÷	6	=	
=		=		=
	+		=	50

2)

3	×		=	30
+		−		÷
10	−		=	
=		=		=
	−	3	=	

3)

15	÷		=	
+		+		×
	−		=	20
=		=		=
45	+		=	60

4)

	−		=	55
÷		÷		−
2	×		=	10
=		=		=
	+	5	=	

5)

	−	4	=	3
+		÷		×
8	+		=	10
=		=		=
	×		=	

6)

	÷	8	=	
÷		−		+
	÷	2	=	5
=		=		=
4	+		=	

7)

	×	6	=	60
+		×		÷
	÷		=	
=		=		=
22	−	12	=	

8)

2	×		=	
×		+		×
	−	8	=	
=		=		=
22	−		=	12

9)

13	+	5	=	
×		−		+
	×	4	=	
=		=		=
26	÷		=	

10)

70	−		−		=	20
÷		÷		−		+
7	+		+	10	=	
=		=		=		=
	+	5	+		=	40

11)

	×	8	=	
+		−		+
	−		=	2
+		−		+
2	×		=	2
=		=		=
12	×	3	=	

12)

	+	4	=	20
+		+		−
32	÷	8	=	
+		−		−
	−		=	6
=		=		=
60	÷		=	

Name: _____

Score:

Make Your Own

Making your own cross-number puzzle may sound simple but can be a challenging task. You may want to trace the cross-number templates onto another sheet of paper to practice on first. That way, you can experiment, erase, and rewrite numbers until you create the puzzle you want.

Helpful Tips

- Fill in the numbers and operations one number sentence at a time.
- Make sure all the number sentence rows and columns are true.
- If number sentences are not true, figure out which numbers can be changed to correct them.
- Write lightly because you will likely need to erase and re-write numbers several times.
- If creating a puzzle isn't working, sometimes it helps to erase the entire puzzle and start over.

Create your own cross-number puzzles by filling in some of the boxes and leaving others blank.
Make sure that your puzzles are solvable. All the number sentences need to be true when solved.

1)
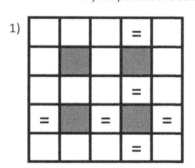

2)
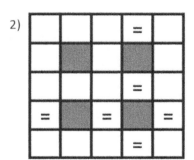

3)
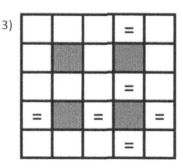

4)
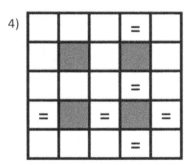

5)
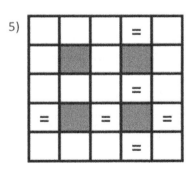

6)
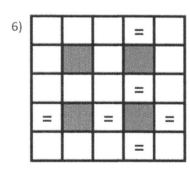

7)
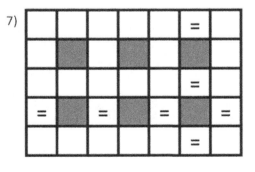

8)
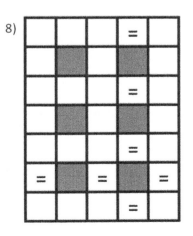

9)
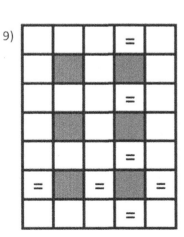

Answers

Day 1:
1) A 2) B 3) B 4) C 5) A

Day 2:
1) C 2) B 3) A 4) B 5) A
6) B 7) A 8) C 9) C 10) A

Day 3:
1) B 2) C 3) C 4) B 5) A
6) C 7) A 8) B 9) C 10) A

Day 4:
1) B 2) A 3) C 4) A 5) C
6) B 7) C 8) B 9) A 10) C

Day 5:
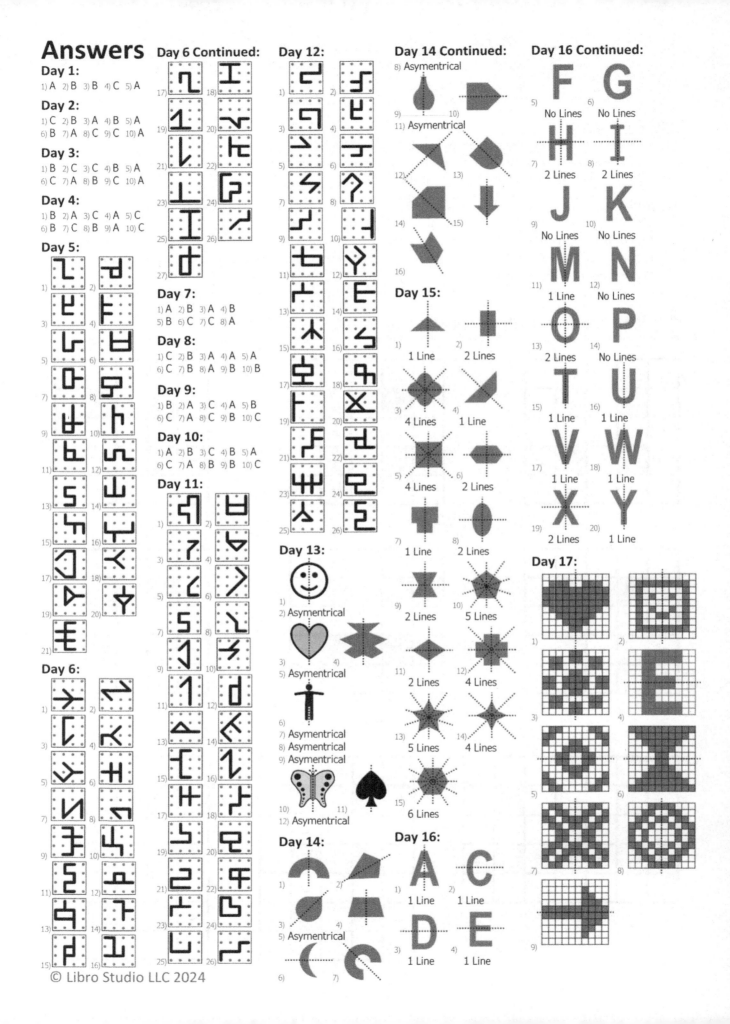

Day 6:

Day 6 Continued:

Day 7:
1) A 2) B 3) A 4) B
5) B 6) C 7) C 8) A

Day 8:
1) C 2) B 3) A 4) A 5) A
6) C 7) B 8) A 9) B 10) B

Day 9:
1) B 2) A 3) C 4) A 5) B
6) C 7) A 8) C 9) B 10) C

Day 10:
1) A 2) B 3) C 4) B 5) A
6) C 7) A 8) B 9) B 10) C

Day 11:

Day 12:

Day 13:
1)
2) Asymentrical
3)
4)
5) Asymentrical
6)
7) Asymentrical
8) Asymentrical
9) Asymentrical
10) 11)
12) Asymentrical

Day 14:
1) 2)
3) 4)
5) Asymentrical
6) 7)

Day 14 Continued:
8) Asymentrical
9) 10)
11) Asymentrical
12) 13)
14) 15)
16)

Day 15:
1) 1 Line 2) 2 Lines
3) 4 Lines 4) 1 Line
5) 4 Lines 6) 2 Lines
7) 1 Line 8) 2 Lines
9) 2 Lines 10) 5 Lines
11) 2 Lines 12) 4 Lines
13) 5 Lines 14) 4 Lines
15) 6 Lines

Day 16:
1) A 1 Line 2) C 1 Line
3) D 1 Line 4) E 1 Line

Day 16 Continued:
F G
5) No Lines 6) No Lines
H I
7) 2 Lines 8) 2 Lines
J K
9) No Lines 10) No Lines
M N
11) 1 Line 12) No Lines
O P
13) 2 Lines 14) No Lines
T U
15) 1 Line 16) 1 Line
V W
17) 1 Line 18) 1 Line
X Y
19) 2 Lines 20) 1 Line

Day 17:
1) 2)
3) 4)
5) 6)
7) 8)
9)

© Libro Studio LLC 2024

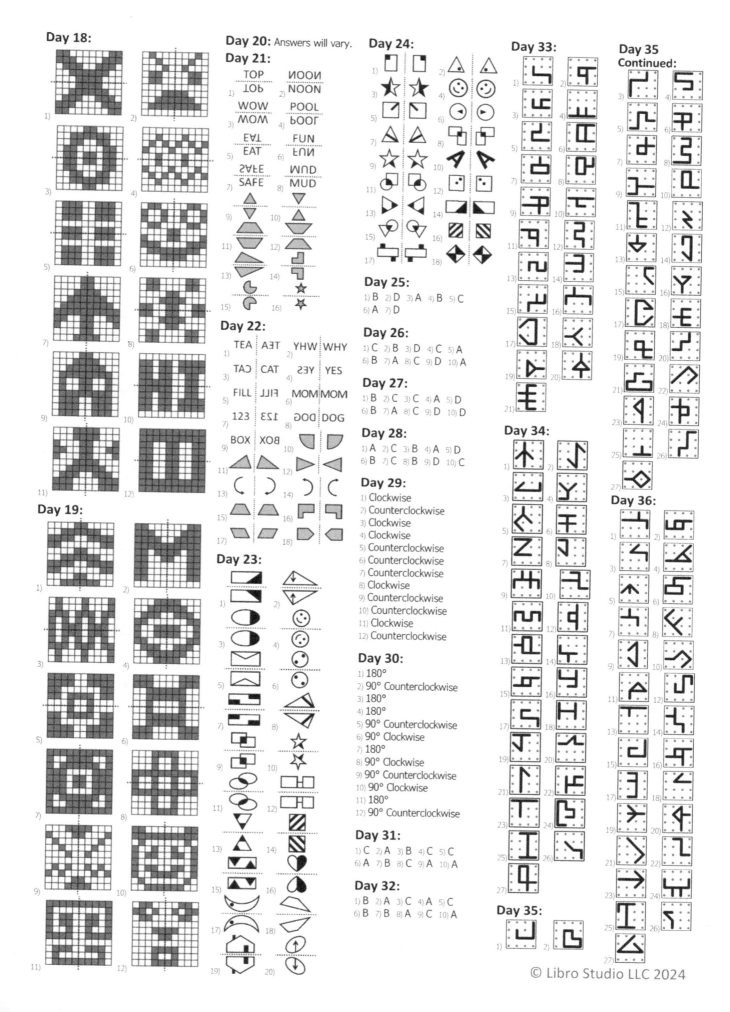

Day 18:

Day 19:

Day 20: Answers will vary.

Day 21:

1) TOP / NOON
3) WOW / POOL
5) EAT / FUN
7) SAFE / MUD

Day 22:

1) TEA 2) WHY
3) CAT 4) YES
5) FILL 6) MOM
7) 123 8) DOG
9) BOX

Day 23:

Day 24:

Day 25:

1) B 2) D 3) A 4) B 5) C
6) A 7) D

Day 26:

1) C 2) B 3) D 4) C 5) A
6) B 7) A 8) C 9) D 10) A

Day 27:

1) B 2) C 3) C 4) A 5) D
6) B 7) A 8) C 9) D 10) D

Day 28:

1) A 2) C 3) B 4) A 5) D
6) B 7) C 8) B 9) D 10) C

Day 29:

1) Clockwise
2) Counterclockwise
3) Clockwise
4) Clockwise
5) Counterclockwise
6) Counterclockwise
7) Counterclockwise
8) Clockwise
9) Counterclockwise
10) Counterclockwise
11) Clockwise
12) Counterclockwise

Day 30:

1) 180°
2) 90° Counterclockwise
3) 180°
4) 180°
5) 90° Counterclockwise
6) 90° Clockwise
7) 180°
8) 90° Clockwise
9) 90° Counterclockwise
10) 90° Clockwise
11) 180°
12) 90° Counterclockwise

Day 31:

1) C 2) A 3) B 4) C 5) C
6) A 7) B 8) C 9) A 10) A

Day 32:

1) B 2) A 3) C 4) A 5) C
6) B 7) B 8) A 9) C 10) A

Day 33:

Day 34:

Day 35:

Day 35 Continued:

Day 36:

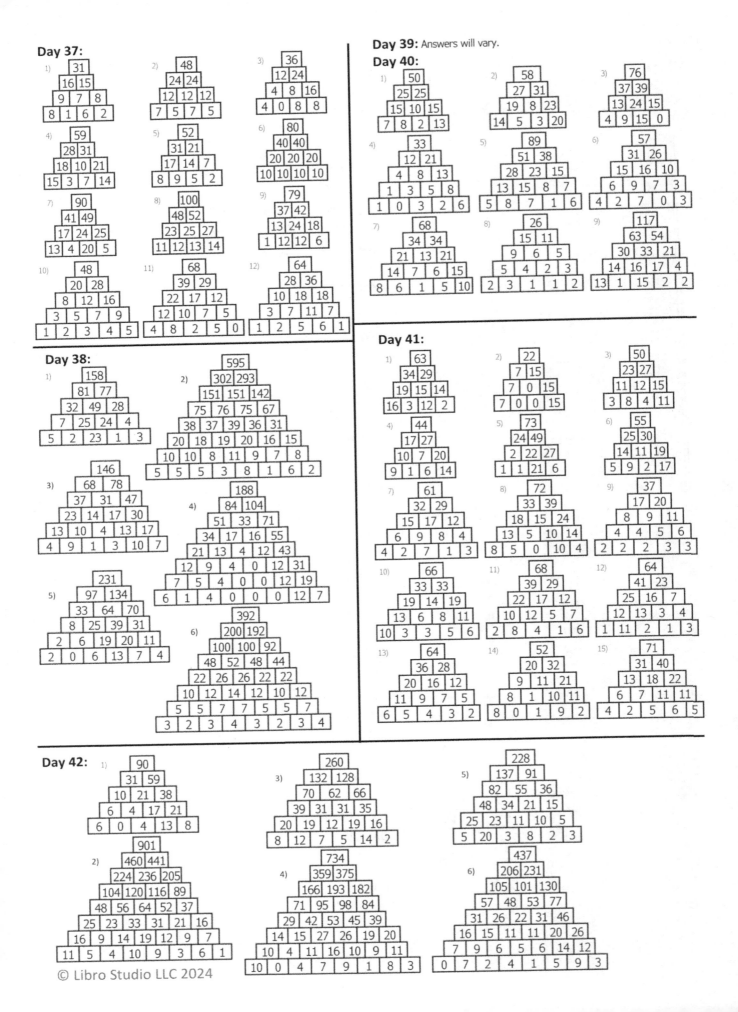

Day 37:

1)
```
      31
    16 15
   9  7  8
  8  1  6  2
```

2)
```
      48
    24 24
  12 12 12
  7  5  7  5
```

3)
```
      36
    12 24
   4  8 16
  4  0  8  8
```

4)
```
      59
    28 31
  18 10 21
 15  3  7 14
```

5)
```
      52
    31 21
  17 14  7
  8  9  5  2
```

6)
```
      80
    40 40
  20 20 20
 10 10 10 10
```

7)
```
      90
    41 49
  17 24 25
 13  4 20  5
```

8)
```
      100
    48 52
  23 25 27
 11 12 13 14
```

9)
```
      79
    37 42
  13 24 18
  1 12 12  6
```

10)
```
        48
      20 28
    8 12 16
   3  5  7  9
  1  2  3  4  5
```

11)
```
        68
      39 29
   22 17 12
  12 10  7  5
  4  8  2  5  0
```

12)
```
        64
      28 36
   10 18 18
   3  7 11  7
  1  2  5  6  1
```

Day 38:

1)
```
        158
      81 77
   32 49 28
   7 25 24  4
  5  2 23  1  3
```

2)
```
            595
        302 293
     151 151 142
    75 76 75 67
   38 37 39 36 31
  20 18 19 20 16 15
 10 10  8 11  9  7  8
5  5  5  3  8  1  6  2
```

3)
```
          146
       68 78
    37 31 47
   23 14 17 30
  13 10  4 13 17
  4  9  1  3 10  7
```

4)
```
            188
        84 104
     51 33 71
    34 17 16 55
   21 13  4 12 43
  12  9  4  0 12 31
 7  5  4  0  0 12 19
6  1  4  0  0  0 12  7
```

5)
```
          231
       97 134
    33 64 70
   8 25 39 31
  2  6 19 20 11
  2  0  6 13  7  4
```

6)
```
            392
        200 192
     100 100 92
    48 52 48 44
   22 26 26 22 22
  10 12 14 12 10 12
 5  5  7  5  5  7
3  2  3  4  3  2  3  4
```

Day 39: Answers will vary.

Day 40:

1)
```
      50
    25 25
  15 10 15
  7  8  2 13
```

2)
```
      58
    27 31
  19  8 23
 14  5  3 20
```

3)
```
      76
    37 39
  13 24 15
  4  9 15  0
```

4)
```
        33
      12 21
    4  8 13
   1  3  5  8
  1  0  3  2  6
```

5)
```
        89
      51 38
   28 23 15
  13 15  8  7
  5  8  7  1  6
```

6)
```
        57
      31 26
   15 16 10
   6  9  7  3
  4  2  7  0  3
```

7)
```
        68
      34 34
   21 13 21
  14  7  6 15
  8  6  1  5 10
```

8)
```
        26
      15 11
    9  6  5
   5  4  2  3
  2  3  1  1  2
```

9)
```
        117
      63 54
   30 33 21
  14 16 17  4
 13  1 15  2  2
```

Day 41:

1)
```
      63
    34 29
  19 15 14
 16  3 12  2
```

2)
```
      22
    7 15
  7  0 15
 7  0  0 15
```

3)
```
      50
    23 27
  11 12 15
  3  8  4 11
```

4)
```
      44
    17 27
  10  7 20
  9  1  6 14
```

5)
```
      73
    24 49
  2 22 27
 1  1 21  6
```

6)
```
      55
    25 30
  14 11 19
  5  9  2 17
```

7)
```
        61
      32 29
   15 17 12
   6  9  8  4
  4  2  7  1  3
```

8)
```
        72
      33 39
   18 15 24
  13  5 10 14
  8  5  0 10  4
```

9)
```
        37
      17 20
    8  9 11
   4  4  5  6
  2  2  2  3  3
```

10)
```
        66
      33 33
   19 14 19
  13  6  8 11
 10  3  3  5  6
```

11)
```
        68
      39 29
   22 17 12
  10 12  5  7
  2  8  4  1  6
```

12)
```
        64
      41 23
   25 16  7
  12 13  3  4
  1 11  2  1  3
```

13)
```
        64
      36 28
   20 16 12
  11  9  7  5
  6  5  4  3  2
```

14)
```
        52
      20 32
    9 11 21
   8  1 10 11
  8  0  1  9  2
```

15)
```
        71
      31 40
   13 18 22
   6  7 11 11
  4  2  5  6  5
```

Day 42:

1)
```
        90
      31 59
   10 21 38
   6  4 17 21
  6  0  4 13  8
```

2)
```
            901
       460 441
    224 236 205
   104 120 116 89
   48 56 64 52 37
  25 23 33 31 21 16
 16  9 14 19 12  9  7
11  5  4 10  9  3  6  1
```

3)
```
          260
      132 128
    70 62 66
   39 31 31 35
  20 19 12 19 16
 8 12  7  5 14  2
```

4)
```
            734
       359 375
    166 193 182
   71 95 98 84
   29 42 53 45 39
  14 15 27 26 19 20
 10  4 11 16 10  9 11
10  0  4  7  9  1  8  3
```

5)
```
          228
      137 91
    82 55 36
   48 34 21 15
  25 23 11 10  5
 5 20  3  8  2  3
```

6)
```
            437
       206 231
    105 101 130
   57 48 53 77
   31 26 22 31 46
  16 15 11 11 20 26
 7  9  6  5  6 14 12
0  7  2  4  1  5  9  3
```

© Libro Studio LLC 2024

Day 43:

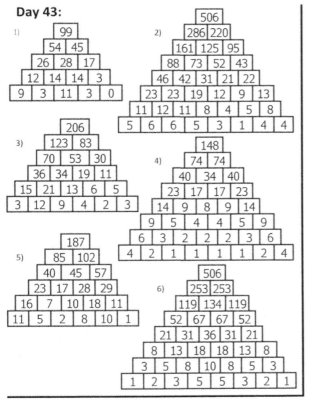

Day 44: Answers will vary.

Day 45:

1) 34, 38, Add 4
2) 65, 70, Add 5
3) 50, 49, Subtract 1
4) 50, 44, Subtract 6
5) 25, 23, Subtract 2
6) 77, 80, Add 3
7) 63, 73, Add 10
8) 14, 6, Subtract 8
9) 95, 97, Add 2
10) 33, 30, Subtract 3
11) 78, 84, Add 6
12) 89, 94, Add 5
13) 15, 4, Subtract 11

Day 46:

1) G 2) A 3) A 4) G 5) A
6) G 7) A 8) G 9) G 10) A

Day 47:

1) Divide by 2 2) Multiply by 10
3) Multiply by 2 4) Divide by 3
5) Divide by 5 6) Multiply by 2
7) Divide by 4 8) Divide by 2
9) Multiply by 5 10) Divide by 3
11) Divide by 4 12) Multiply by 5
13) Divide by 6 14) Divide by 10
15) Multiply by 3 16) Multiply by 2

Day 48:

1) Divide by 3, 108, 36
2) Divide by 5, 35, 7
3) Multiply by 4, 3,072, 12,288
4) Multiply by 3, 3,159, 9,477
5) Divide by 2, 480, 240
6) Multiply by 5, 5,000, 25,000
7) Multiply by 2, 1,472, 2,944
8) Divide by 4, 56, 14
9) Multiply by 6, 54,432, 326,592
10) Divide by 3, 48, 16
11) Divide by 2, 104, 52
12) Multiply by 3, 4,131, 12,393

Day 49:

1) Multiply by 5, 18,750, 93,750
2) Divide by 2, 76, 38
3) Multiply by 8, 12,288, 98,304
4) Divide by 6, 42, 7
5) Divide by 4, 144, 36
6) Multiply by 2, 640, 1,280
7) Divide by 3, 297, 99
8) Multiply by 4, 13,312, 53,248
9) Multiply by 6, 54,432, 326,592
10) Divide by 5, 150, 30
11) Divide by 2, 168, 84
12) Multiply by 3, 3,888, 11,664
13) Divide by 4, 64, 16
14) Multiply by 10, 30,000, 300,000
15) Divide by 7, 21, 3
16) Multiply by 2, 832, 1,664
17) Multiply by 3, 3,159, 9,477
18) Divide by 2, 200, 100

Day 50:

1) Add 23, 143, 166
2) Multiply by 2, 928, 1,856
3) Divide by 3, 225, 75
4) Subtract 35, 387, 352
5) Divide by 2, 328, 164
6) Add 68, 1,174, 1,242
7) Divide by 5, 400, 80
8) Subtract 125, 3,767, 3,642
9) Multiply by 4, 17,408, 69,632
10) Divide by 3, 513, 171
11) Subtract 47, 9,994, 9,947
12) Add by 605, 4,779 , 5,384
13) Divide by 2, 344, 172
14) Subtract by 1,200, 5,092, 3,892
15) Multiply by 5, 37,500, 187,500
16) Divide by 6, 30, 5

Day 51:

1) Subtract 95, 868, 773
2) Multiply by 3, 2,754, 8,262
3) Add 252, 4,788, 5,040
4) Subtract 1,184, 7,645, 6,461
5) Divide by 2, 424, 212

Day 51 Continued:

6) Divide by 4, 108, 27
7) Multiply by 5, 11,875, 59,375
8) Add 2,086, 11,412, 13,498
9) Multiply by 2, 3,488, 6,976
10) Multiply by 2, 10,032, 20,064
11) Subtract 582, 14,926, 14,344
12) Add by 394, 5,137, 5,531
13) Divide by 3, 324, 108
14) Add by 4,670, 19,263, 23,933
15) Multiply by 4, 15,360, 61,440
16) Subtract by 3,472, 6,463, 2,991
17) Divide by 5, 105, 21
18) Add by 4,608, 50,848, 55,456

Day 52:

1) 910, 1,038 (Add 64)
2) 75, 1,200 (Multiply by 2)
3) 144, 11,664 (Multiply by 3)
4) 4,509, 4,405 (Subtract 52)
5) 1,125, 28,125 (Multiply by 5)
6) 2,003, 1,829 (Subtract 174)
7) 3,008, 94 (Divide by 2)
8) 7,922, 8,980 (Add 529)
9) 89,088, 22,272 (Divide by 4)
10) 8, 19,208 (Multiply by 7)
11) 8,181, 7,198 (Subtract 983)
12) 1,033, 663 (Subtract 74)
13) 1,008, 126 (Divide by 2)

Day 53:

1) 6,162, 4,770 (Subtract 348)
2) 6, 600 (Multiply by 10)
3) 8,269, 9,833 (Add 782)
4) 126, 30,618 (Multiply by 3)
5) 35,840, 140 (Divide by 4)
6) 10,125, 1,873 (Subtract 2,063)
7) 353, 11,296 (Multiply by 2)
8) 8,323, 12,131 (Add 1,904)
9) 5,427, 201 (Divide by 3)
10) 4,794, 3,960 (Subtract 417)
11) 3,520, 14,080 (Multiply by 4)
12) 965, 1,053 (Add 88)
13) 21,954, 17,673 (Subtract 4,281)
14) 4,576, 1,144 (Divide by 2)

Day 54:

1) 49, 50,176 (Multiply by 4)
2) 325, 65 (Divide by 5)
3) 4,898, 4,547 (Subtract 351)
4) 96, 124,416 (Multiply by 6)
5) 3,735, 10,897 (Add 3,581)
6) 20,544, 642 (Divide by 2)
7) 1,459, 2,273 (Add 814)
8) 121, 1,089 (Multiply by 3)
9) 9,797, 6,913 (Subtract 721)
10) 37,908, 4,212 (Divide by 3)
11) 15,616, 61 (Divide by 4)
12) 3,147, 15,922 (Add 2,555)
13) 2,344, 9,376 (Multiply by 2)
14) 890, 534 (Subtract 89)

Day 55:

1) 5,671, 4,711 (Subtract 192)
2) 19,023, 8,955 (Subtract 2,517)
3) 3,616, 14,464 (Multiply by 2)
4) 900,000, 9,000 (Divide by 10)
5) 435, 54,375 (Multiply by 5)
6) 672, 21,592 (Add 4,184)
7) 22,528, 88 (Divide by 4)
8) 7,729, 6,769 (Subtract 480)
9) 1,305, 3,915 (Multiply by 3)
10) 7,079, 4,597 (Subtract 1,241)
11) 2,355, 2,968 (Add 613)
12) 4,240, 2,120 (Divide by 2)
13) 576, 36,864 (Multiply by 8)
14) 11,937, 34,813 (Add 5,719)

Day 56:

1) 57, 13,851 (Multiply by 3)
2) 9,640, 7,764 (Subtract 938)
3) 2,688, 672 (Divide by 4)
4) 6,480, 7,783 (Add 1,303)
5) 9,619, 11,043 (Add 712)
6) 1,928, 482 (Divide by 2)
7) 21,396, 17,228 (Subtract 2,084)
8) 85, 10,625 (Multiply by 5)
9) 26,244, 8,748 (Divide by 3)
10) 1,342, 21,472 (Multiply by 2)
11) 7,860, 5,045 (Subtract 563)
12) 2,268, 252 (Divide by 3)
13) 3,204, 6,172 (Add 742)
14) 19, 684 (Multiply by 6)

Day 57:

1) Subtract 2 2) Subtract 1
3) Subtract 1 4) Add 4 5) Add 1

Day 58:

1) Add 5, 79, 107
2) Subtract 3, 45, 25
3) Subtract 2, 80, 66
4) Add 1, 147, 153
5) Add 6, 79, 112
6) Subtract 2, 103, 113
7) Add 1, 70, 67
8) Subtract 5, 210, 185
9) Subtract 1, 101, 105
10) Add 2, 372, 388

Day 59:

1) Subtract 3, 425, 431
2) Add 1, 106, 115
3) Subtract 6, 358, 322
4) Subtract 1, 59, 52
5) Add 4, 125, 155
6) Add 2, 142, 163
7) Subtract 2, 74, 60
8) Add 3, 604, 593
9) Subtract 5, 212, 232
10) Add 1, 995, 1,005
11) Add 7, 545, 540
12) Subtract 4, 592, 571

Day 60:

1) Add 1, 381, 376
2) Add 4, 232, 250
3) Subtract 2, 200, 214
4) Add 10, 631, 686
5) Subtract 3, 662, 750
6) Subtract 1, 67, 59
7) Subtract 4, 722, 694
8) Add 2, 709, 725
9) Add 5, 227, 205
10) Subtract 6, 516, 486
11) Add 8, 177, 216
12) Subtract 2, 58, 43

Day 61:

1) Add 4, 110, 141
2) Subtract 3, 49, 32
3) Add 2, 127, 160
4) Add 2, 203, 187
5) Add 1, 816, 804
6) Subtract 5, 585, 556
7) Subtract 10, 188, 144
8) Add 7, 308, 290
9) Subtract 1, 24, 17
10) Add 4, 454, 481
11) Add 3, 276, 265
12) Subtract 2, 632, 621

Day 62:
1) Subtract 6, 87, 56
2) Add 4, 265, 283
3) Add 9, 431, 476
4) Add 1, 76, 82
5) Add 3, 735, 756
6) Subtract 5, 505, 483
7) Add 2, 788, 776
8) Add 2, 526, 543
9) Subtract 3, 124, 137
10) Subtract 10, 632, 572
11) Add 3, 401, 421
12) Add 5, 430, 390

Day 63:
1) Arithmetic, 349, 355
2) Quadratic, 750, 737
3) Geometric, 405, 1,215
4) Quadratic, 104, 154
5) Arithmetic, 680, 658
6) Geometric, 33, 11
7) Quadratic, 1,000, 400
8) Geometric, 384, 768
9) Quadratic, 265, 310
10) Arithmetic, 493, 525

Day 64:
1) Geometric, 1,296, 3,888
2) Geometric, 20, 5
3) Arithmetic, 477, 534
4) Quadratic, 374, 398
5) Arithmetic, 721, 706
6) Quadratic, 177, 165
7) Geometric, 10, 2
8) Arithmetic, 633, 740
9) Quadratic, 99, 125
10) Geometric, 912, 1,824
11) Arithmetic, 472, 404
12) Quadratic, 195, 174

Day 65:
1) Quadratic, 885, 867
2) Arithmetic, 404, 387
3) Geometric, 3,584, 14,336
4) Geometric 60, 20
5) Quadratic, 122, 111
6) Arithmetic, 749, 783
7) Quadratic, 136, 148
8) Geometric, 146, 73
9) Arithmetic, 81, 52
10) Arithmetic, 499, 592
11) Quadratic, 644, 628
12) Geometric, 2,672, 5,344

Day 66:
1) 125, 253
2) 87, 167
3) 200, 408
4) 258, 744
5) 5,000, 4,500
6) 33, 4
7) 21, 9
8) 55, 25

Day 67
1) Multiply by 2, Subtract 5
2) Multiply by 2, Add 4
3) Add 6, Multiply by 2
4) Subtract 5, Multiply by 3
5) Add 10, Multiply by 2
6) Multiply by 5, Subtract 10
7) Multiply by 3, Add 1
8) Subtract 2, Multiply by 3
9) Add 7, Multiply by 2
10) Multiply by 3, Subtract 40

Day 68:
1) Multiply by 2, Subtract 8, 3,096, 6,184

Day 68 Continued:
2) Add 2, Multiply by 2, 124, 252
3) Multiply by 2, Add 10, 278, 566
4) Subtract 6, Multiply by 3, 90, 252
5) Add 20, Multiply by 2, 648, 1,336
6) Add 1, Multiply by 2, 126, 254
7) Multiply by 2, Subtract 25, 345, 665
8) Multiply by 2, Subtract 5, 277, 549
9) Add 1, Multiply by 4, 2,388, 9,556
10) Multiply by 2, Subtract 100, 1,700, 3,300
11) Multiply by 3, Add 5, 848, 2,549
12) Subtract 10, Multiply by 3, 8,520, 25,530

Day 69:
1) Divide by 2, Subtract 5, 34, 12
2) Divide by 2, Add 3, 510, 258
3) Add 6, Divide by 3, 57, 21
4) Divide by 4, Subtract 10, 72, 8
5) Subtract 50, Divide by 2, 678, 314
6) Divide by 4, Add 100, 424, 206
7) Add 25, Divide by 3, 20, 15
8) Subtract 1, Divide by 3, 133, 44
9) Divide by 2, Subtract 100, 312, 56
10) Divide by 4, Add 200, 1,032, 458
11) Subtract 6, Divide by 2, 20, 7
12) Add 7, Divide by 2, 43, 25

Day 70:
1) 16, 25, 36

2) 19, 29, 41

3) 13, 17, 21

4) 7, 9, 11

5) 9, 11, 13

6) 7, 9, 11

7) 10, 13, 16

8) 6, 7, 8

9) 10, 15, 21

10) 17, 21, 25

Day 71:
1) 10, 13, 16

2) 20, 24, 28

3) 16, 25, 36

4) 8, 10, 12

5) 11, 14, 17

6) 10, 13, 16

7) 10, 12, 14

8) 7, 9, 11

9) 16, 21, 26

10) 12, 14, 16

11) 20, 25, 30

12) 8, 10, 12

Day 71
13) 13, 16, 19

14) 11, 16, 22

Day 72:
1) A 2) C

Day 73:
1) D 2) B 3) C 4) D 5) B

Day 74:
1) A 2) D 3) C 4) A 5) C

Day 75:
1) B 2) C 3) D 4) D 5) B

Day 76:

1) 2)
3) 4)
5) 6)
7) 8)

Day 77:

1) 2)
3) 4)
5) 6)
7) 8)
9) 10)
11) 12)
13) 14)
15) 16)
17) 18)
19) 20)

Day 78:

1) 2)
3) 4)
5) 6)
7) 8)
9) 10)
11) 12)
13) 14)
15) 16)

Day 78 Continued:

13) 14)
15) 16)
17) 18)
19) 20)

Day 79:

1) 2)
3) 4)
5) 6)
7) 8)
9) 10)
11) 12)
13) 14)
15) 16)
17) 18)
19) 20)

Day 80:

1) 2)
3) 4)
5) 6)
7) 8)

Day 81:

1) 2)
3) 4)
5) 6)
7) 8)
9) 10)
11) 12)
13) 14)
15) 16)

Day 81 Continued:

17) 18)
19) 20)

Day 82:

1) 2)
3) 4)
5) 6)
7) 8)
9) 10)
11) 12)
13) 14)
15) 16)
17) 18)
19) 20)

Day 83:
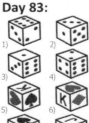
1) 2)
3) 4)
5) 6)
7) 8)
9) 10)
11) 12)
13) 14)
15) 16)
17) 18)
19) 20)

Day 84:
1) $5 \times 6 \div 10 = 3$
2) $200 - 50 \times 3 = 450$
3) $100 \div 2 - 10 = 40$
4) $4 + 7 \times 4 = 44$
5) $10 \times 4 \times 3 = 120$
6) $35 - 20 \div 3 = 5$
7) $5 + 10 + 12 = 27$
8) $30 - 5 \times 4 = 100$
9) $100 \div 5 \times 4 = 80$

Day 84 Continued:

10) $50 \times 4 \times 3 = 600$
11) $60 \div 5 - 3 = 9$
12) $80 + 20 + 10 = 110$
13) $500 \times 2 \div 10 = 100$
14) $8 \times 4 - 6 = 26$
15) $20 \div 5 \times 7 = 28$
16) $7 - 5 \times 15 = 30$
17) $50 - 20 - 4 = 26$
18) $60 - 15 \div 9 = 5$
19) $4 \times 3 + 3 = 15$
20) $10 \div 10 + 5 = 6$
21) $8 - 6 + 1 = 3$
22) $10 - 5 \times 5 = 25$
23) $10 \div 5 + 5 = 7$
24) $10 \times 5 + 5 = 55$
25) $10 \times 5 \times 5 = 250$
26) $10 \times 5 - 5 = 45$

Day 85:

1) $9 \div 3 + 3 = 6$
2) $9 \times 3 + 3 = 30$
3) $9 - 3 - 3 = 3$
4) $9 \div 3 \div 3 = 1$
5) $100 \times 4 \div 10 = 40$
6) $100 \div 4 \times 10 = 250$
7) $100 \div 4 + 10 = 35$
8) $100 - 4 \times 10 = 960$
9) $100 \times 4 - 10 = 390$
10) $24 \times 2 - 5 = 43$
11) $24 \div 2 \times 5 = 60$
12) $24 - 2 \times 5 = 110$
13) $40 + 5 \div 3 = 15$
14) $40 \div 5 - 3 = 5$
15) $40 - 5 \times 3 = 105$
16) $12 + 2 \times 10 = 140$
17) $12 \times 2 \times 10 = 240$
18) $12 \div 2 + 10 = 16$
19) $12 - 2 \times 10 = 100$
20) $20 \times 4 \div 2 = 40$
21) $20 \div 4 \times 2 = 10$
22) $20 + 4 \div 2 = 12$
23) $20 \div 4 - 2 = 3$
24) $60 \div 12 \times 5 = 25$
25) $60 - 12 + 5 = 53$
26) $200 \times 5 \div 10 = 100$
27) $200 \div 5 \div 10 = 4$
28) $200 - 5 - 10 = 185$
29) $200 \times 5 \times 10 = 10,000$
30) $200 - 5 \times 10 = 1,950$

Day 86:

1) $5 + 6 \times 2 + 4 = 26$
2) $7 \times 3 - 4 - 10 = 7$
3) $3 \times 8 - 20 + 5 = 9$
4) $20 \div 4 \times 9 - 40 = 5$
5) $2 + 8 \div 5 \times 3 = 6$
6) $36 \div 6 \div 2 + 7 = 10$
7) $14 - 6 - 2 \div 3 = 2$
8) $6 + 1 \times 5 - 10 = 25$
9) $9 + 7 + 6 \times 2 = 44$
10) $8 \times 5 - 15 \div 5 = 5$
11) $80 - 40 - 20 + 7 = 27$
12) $18 \div 6 + 8 - 2 = 9$
13) $1 + 1 + 3 \times 4 = 20$
14) $24 \div 4 \div 3 \times 7 = 14$
15) $4 \times 7 - 6 \div 2 = 11$
16) $90 \div 10 \div 3 + 17 = 20$

Day 86 Continued:

17) $4 \times 3 - 1 - 7 = 4$
18) $5 \times 4 \div 2 - 8 = 2$
19) $3 + 6 - 2 + 5 = 12$
20) $100 \div 20 \times 9 + 5 = 50$
21) $50 - 20 + 10 \times 3 = 120$
22) $2 \times 3 + 4 \times 12 = 120$
23) $8 \div 4 + 7 \div 3 = 3$
24) $9 + 6 - 5 \times 8 = 80$
25) $60 - 30 \div 10 + 2 = 5$
26) $1 \times 2 + 4 \times 6 = 36$

Day 87:

1) $8 + 2 - 5 \times 3 = 15$
2) $120 \div 10 + 3 - 6 = 9$
3) $4 \times 7 \div 28 + 3 = 4$
4) $9 - 5 \times 3 \div 2 = 6$
5) $100 \div 4 \times 2 - 25 = 25$
6) $4 \times 5 - 4 + 6 = 22$
7) $10 - 3 + 9 \div 16 = 1$
8) $9 + 4 + 3 - 5 = 11$
9) $6 \times 2 \times 2 \div 8 = 3$
10) $7 - 4 - 2 \times 200 = 200$
11) $50 \div 10 \div 5 + 40 = 41$
12) $3 + 7 - 8 \times 9 = 18$
13) $15 - 5 \times 20 - 40 = 160$
14) $6 \times 7 \div 42 + 6 = 7$
15) $24 \div 2 + 8 - 5 = 15$
16) $9 \times 2 - 12 + 4 = 10$
17) $70 + 30 + 60 \div 4 = 40$
18) $11 - 6 \times 4 - 1 = 19$
19) $2 \times 4 \div 8 + 99 = 100$
20) $30 \div 3 + 13 + 5 = 28$
21) $4 \times 10 \times 2 + 30 = 110$
22) $6 \div 2 + 12 \div 5 = 3$
23) $81 \div 9 + 1 \div 2 = 5$
24) $3 + 9 \times 10 + 20 = 140$
25) $75 - 70 + 5 \times 5 = 50$
26) $3 \times 7 + 7 \div 2 = 14$
27) $9 \times 5 - 15 \div 10 = 3$
28) $5 + 9 \times 2 + 4 = 32$
29) $7 \times 5 - 1 + 4 = 38$
30) $9 - 5 \times 6 \div 8 = 3$

Day 88:

1) $60 \div 30 \times 5 \times 4 = 40$
2) $11 - 6 \times 8 + 1 = 41$
3) $5 \times 8 \times 3 + 5 = 125$
4) $9 \times 3 - 20 \div 7 = 1$
5) $7 \times 4 - 3 \times 2 = 50$
6) $4 \times 5 - 4 + 6 = 22$
7) $18 \div 2 - 7 - 1 = 1$
8) $5 - 4 + 3 + 8 = 12$
9) $8 - 5 \times 4 - 2 = 10$
10) $2 + 6 + 5 - 7 = 6$
11) $87 - 7 \div 8 \times 2 = 20$
12) $2 \times 25 - 2 \div 6 = 8$
13) $7 \times 5 + 5 - 1 = 39$
14) $8 \div 8 + 6 \times 4 = 28$
15) $10 - 7 \times 8 \div 2 = 12$
16) $1 \times 9 + 2 - 8 = 3$
17) $2 + 4 \times 6 \times 3 = 108$
18) $62 - 7 \div 5 + 1 = 12$
19) $3 \times 6 + 9 + 200 = 227$
20) $500 \div 4 - 3 - 2 = 120$
21) $29 + 9 - 6 \div 4 = 8$
22) $45 \div 15 + 30 - 9 = 24$
23) $8 \times 4 - 12 + 7 = 27$

Day 88 Continued:

24) $16 - 6 \times 3 \div 5 = 6$
25) $7 \times 5 - 6 + 2 = 31$
26) $60 \div 20 \times 4 + 5 = 17$
27) $90 + 70 \div 40 \times 11 = 44$
28) $8 \times 5 \times 6 - 90 = 150$
29) $3 - 1 + 6 \times 4 = 32$
30) $250 + 50 + 50 \div 7 = 50$

Day 89:

1) $1,000 \div 20 + 10 - 5 = 55$
2) $7 \times 5 \times 2 + 3 = 73$
3) $96 - 6 + 40 \div 13 = 10$
4) $8 + 1 - 3 \times 5 = 30$
5) $4 \times 9 - 7 - 6 = 23$
6) $25 \div 5 + 9 + 1 = 15$
7) $6 + 3 + 3 \times 4 = 48$
8) $900 - 600 - 50 \div 250 = 1$
9) $36 + 24 \div 15 + 2 = 6$
10) $88 - 80 \times 4 + 6 = 38$
11) $5 + 15 \div 4 \times 8 = 40$
12) $9 - 3 \times 5 \times 3 = 90$
13) $4 \times 6 + 6 \div 3 = 10$
14) $70 + 20 \times 3 - 70 = 200$
15) $120 - 50 \div 70 + 16 = 17$
16) $144 \div 12 + 3 \times 5 = 75$
17) $2 \times 20 - 10 \times 2 = 60$
18) $700 - 300 \div 50 - 4 = 4$
19) $39 + 1 \times 12 + 20 = 500$
20) $16 \div 4 + 24 \div 2 = 14$
21) $19 + 17 + 8 \div 4 = 11$
22) $24 \times 4 - 16 + 20 = 100$
23) $80 \div 5 \times 3 + 9 = 57$
24) $5 + 6 - 7 + 8 = 12$
25) $24 \times 4 + 3 \div 9 = 11$
26) $98 + 7 - 90 \times 4 = 60$
27) $6 - 1 + 10 \div 3 = 5$
28) $9 + 4 - 8 \times 5 = 25$
29) $1 \times 9 \times 5 + 5 = 50$
30) $8 + 6 \times 7 - 8 = 90$

Day 90:

1) $15 \div 3 \times 7 - 10 - 1 = 24$
2) $9 + 6 \times 3 + 1 \div 23 = 2$
3) $7 - 5 \times 10 \times 2 \div 5 = 8$
4) $6 \times 5 \times 4 \div 3 - 10 = 30$
5) $4 \times 4 - 5 + 17 + 9 = 37$
6) $30 \div 2 - 5 - 4 \div 2 = 3$
7) $1 + 76 \div 11 - 3 \times 8 = 32$
8) $2 - 1 \times 66 + 34 \div 20 = 5$
9) $8 \times 5 \div 4 - 7 + 4 = 7$
10) $3 + 11 - 7 \div 7 \times 71 = 71$
11) $99 \div 9 + 4 + 35 \div 10 = 5$
12) $7 \times 2 - 3 \times 4 - 7 = 37$
13) $8 + 5 + 7 \div 10 \times 15 = 30$
14) $16 \div 4 \times 5 - 6 + 8 = 22$
15) $4 \times 2 + 72 - 50 \times 3 = 90$
16) $6 + 7 + 7 - 4 + 2 = 18$
17) $57 - 6 - 18 + 4 \times 5 = 185$
18) $9 + 31 \div 2 + 8 \div 4 = 7$
19) $14 \div 7 + 8 - 6 \times 9 = 36$
20) $2 \times 5 - 4 \div 3 + 66 = 68$
21) $48 - 16 \div 8 + 1 + 6 = 11$
22) $3 + 51 + 9 - 13 \div 2 = 25$
23) $7 \times 6 + 8 \div 2 - 13 = 12$
24) $9 + 6 \times 10 - 70 + 30 = 110$
25) $1 \times 50 + 20 - 16 - 14 = 40$
26) $36 \div 6 \times 8 - 12 - 9 = 27$

Day 91:

1) $10 - 8 \times 5 = 10$
2) $9 \times 4 - 3 = 33$
   or $4 \times 9 - 3 = 33$
3) $7 \times 2 - 4 = 10$
   or $2 \times 7 - 4 = 10$
4) $11 - 3 \times 9 = 72$
5) $20 \div 4 - 2 = 3$
6) $15 + 6 \div 3 = 7$
   or $6 + 15 \div 3 = 7$
7) $30 - 8 \div 2 = 11$
8) $40 \div 20 \times 50 = 100$
   or $40 \times 50 \div 20 = 100$
9) $5 \times 4 + 40 = 60$
   or $4 \times 5 + 40 = 60$
10) $3 \times 25 - 30 = 45$
   or $25 \times 3 - 30 = 45$
11) $6 + 10 \div 2 = 8$
   or $10 + 6 \div 2 = 8$
12) $40 \div 4 - 5 = 5$
13) $40 - 20 - 5 = 15$
   or $40 - 5 - 20 = 15$
14) $18 \div 6 - 2 = 1$
15) $2 \times 24 - 10 = 38$
   or $24 \times 2 - 10 = 38$

Day 92:

1) $2 + 5 - 4 = 3$
   or $5 + 2 - 4 = 3$
2) $10 + 20 \div 5 = 6$
   or $20 + 10 \div 5 = 6$
3) $4 \times 12 + 6 = 54$
   or $12 \times 4 + 6 = 54$
4) $8 + 10 \div 2 = 9$
   or $10 + 8 \div 2 = 9$
5) $11 - 6 \times 4 = 20$
6) $24 - 9 - 2 = 13$
7) $18 \div 3 \times 2 = 12$
8) $50 \div 10 \times 5 = 25$

Day 93:

1) $25 - 7 \div 3 = 6$
2) $12 \div 4 + 2 = 5$
3) $13 - 9 \times 7 = 28$
4) $11 + 5 \div 8 = 2$
   or $5 + 11 \div 8 = 2$
5) $4 \times 2 + 5 = 13$
   or $2 \times 4 + 5 = 13$
6) $11 + 4 \times 3 = 45$
   or $4 + 11 \times 3 = 45$
7) $5 - 1 \times 6 = 24$
8) $6 \times 4 \div 12 = 2$
   or $4 \times 6 \div 12 = 2$
9) $18 \div 2 + 1 = 10$
10) $6 - 4 \times 13 = 26$
11) $6 \div 2 \times 7 = 21$
12) $7 \times 2 - 3 = 11$
   or $2 \times 7 - 3 = 11$

Day 94:

1)

7	6	9	8	4	3	1	2	5
8	2	3	7	1	5	4	6	9
4	1	5	6	2	9	3	8	7
6	9	4	3	5	1	2	7	8
3	8	1	2	7	6	9	5	4
2	5	7	9	8	4	6	3	1
5	3	8	1	9	2	7	4	6
1	4	2	5	6	7	8	9	3
9	7	6	4	3	8	5	1	2

2)

9	1	2	7	6	5	3	8	4
5	6	3	8	9	4	7	2	1
7	4	8	1	2	3	9	6	5
8	3	9	6	1	2	5	4	7
1	5	6	9	4	7	2	3	8
2	7	4	3	5	8	6	1	9
4	8	5	2	3	9	1	7	6
6	2	7	5	8	1	4	9	3
3	9	1	4	7	6	8	5	2

Day 95:

1)

4	9	7	6	5	3	8	1	2
8	6	3	1	2	7	4	9	5
5	2	1	8	4	9	6	3	7
7	4	6	2	1	5	9	8	3
3	8	9	7	6	4	2	5	1
1	5	2	9	3	8	7	6	4
2	1	4	5	8	6	3	7	9
6	7	5	3	9	2	1	4	8
9	3	8	4	7	1	5	2	6

2)

4	8	7	5	6	9	1	3	2
9	5	6	2	1	3	7	4	8
3	2	1	8	7	4	6	9	5
5	6	9	1	3	2	4	8	7
2	1	3	7	4	8	9	5	6
8	7	4	6	9	5	3	2	1
1	3	2	4	8	7	5	6	9
7	4	8	9	5	6	2	1	3
6	9	5	3	2	1	8	7	4

3)

9	2	7	1	4	3	6	8	5
1	3	6	5	8	2	7	4	9
5	8	4	9	7	6	1	3	2
6	1	3	2	5	9	8	7	4
7	9	2	4	6	8	3	5	1
4	5	8	7	3	1	2	9	6
8	4	5	6	2	7	9	1	3
3	6	1	8	9	4	5	2	7
2	7	9	3	1	5	4	6	8

4)

5	7	2	8	6	3	4	1	9
4	8	3	1	9	2	5	7	6
6	9	1	4	5	7	8	3	2
2	5	8	9	1	6	7	4	3
3	4	7	2	8	5	9	6	1
1	6	9	7	3	4	2	8	5
9	1	5	6	4	8	3	2	7
8	2	6	3	7	9	1	5	4
7	3	4	5	2	1	6	9	8

Day 96:

1)

7	5	9	1	8	3	6	4	2
8	2	1	5	6	4	3	7	9
3	6	4	7	2	9	5	8	1
4	3	2	9	5	8	1	6	7
6	7	8	3	1	2	9	5	4
1	9	5	4	7	6	2	3	8
2	8	3	6	4	1	7	9	5
9	1	7	8	3	5	4	2	6
5	4	6	2	9	7	8	1	3

2)

9	1	5	8	2	7	3	6	4
4	8	7	3	1	6	9	5	2
3	2	6	5	9	4	8	7	1
5	3	1	7	4	2	6	9	8
7	4	8	6	3	9	2	1	5
2	6	9	1	5	8	4	3	7
6	7	3	2	8	5	1	4	9
8	5	4	9	6	1	7	2	3
1	9	2	4	7	3	5	8	6

3)

1	2	3	5	8	4	9	6	7
8	7	5	6	9	3	2	4	1
9	4	6	7	2	1	3	8	5
7	3	2	4	5	6	1	9	8
6	9	8	2	1	7	5	3	4
5	1	4	8	3	9	6	7	2
3	8	9	1	4	5	7	2	6
4	5	7	9	6	2	8	1	3
2	6	1	3	7	8	4	5	9

4)

4	5	2	3	8	9	7	6	1
8	9	3	6	1	7	5	2	4
1	7	6	2	4	5	9	3	8
3	8	9	7	6	1	4	5	2
6	1	7	5	2	4	8	9	3
2	4	5	9	3	8	1	7	6
7	6	1	4	5	2	3	8	9
5	2	4	8	9	3	6	1	7
9	3	8	1	7	6	2	4	5

Day 97:

1)
$$18 - 0 = 18$$
$$+ \quad + \quad +$$
$$6 + 1 = 7$$
$$= \quad = \quad =$$
$$24 + 1 = 25$$

2)
$$17 + 24 = 41$$
$$+ \quad + \quad +$$
$$31 + 5 = 36$$
$$= \quad = \quad =$$
$$48 + 29 = 77$$

3)
$$16 + 12 = 28$$
$$+ \quad - \quad +$$
$$15 - 12 = 3$$
$$= \quad = \quad =$$
$$31 + 0 = 31$$

4)
$$45 - 28 = 17$$
$$- \quad - \quad +$$
$$26 + 2 = 28$$
$$= \quad = \quad =$$
$$19 + 26 = 45$$

5)
$$29 - 19 = 10$$
$$+ \quad + \quad +$$
$$19 - 11 = 8$$
$$= \quad = \quad =$$
$$48 - 30 = 18$$

6)
$$12 + 60 = 72$$
$$+ \quad - \quad +$$
$$68 - 57 = 11$$
$$= \quad = \quad =$$
$$80 + 3 = 83$$

7)
$$52 + 15 = 67$$
$$- \quad + \quad -$$
$$38 - 28 = 10$$
$$= \quad = \quad =$$
$$14 + 43 = 57$$

8)
$$44 + 37 = 81$$
$$+ \quad - \quad +$$
$$29 - 24 = 5$$
$$= \quad = \quad =$$
$$73 + 13 = 86$$

9)
$$62 - 22 = 40$$
$$- \quad - \quad -$$
$$45 - 22 = 23$$
$$= \quad = \quad =$$
$$17 + 0 = 17$$

Day 98:

1)
$$28 - 7 + 14 = 35$$
$$+ \quad + \quad - \quad +$$
$$7 + 2 + 7 = 16$$
$$= \quad = \quad = \quad =$$
$$35 + 9 + 7 = 51$$

2)
$$80 - 75 + 13 - 13 = 5$$
$$+ \quad - \quad + \quad + \quad +$$
$$19 + 35 - 6 + 20 = 68$$
$$= \quad = \quad = \quad = \quad =$$
$$99 - 40 - 19 + 33 = 73$$

3)
$$45 + 15 + 25 = 85$$
$$- \quad + \quad - \quad -$$
$$25 - 20 + 10 = 15$$
$$= \quad = \quad = \quad =$$
$$20 + 35 + 15 = 70$$

4)
$$6 - 2 = 4$$
$$+ \quad + \quad +$$
$$5 - 1 = 4$$
$$- \quad + \quad +$$
$$3 + 7 = 10$$
$$= \quad = \quad =$$
$$8 + 10 = 18$$

5)
$$18 - 7 = 11$$
$$+ \quad - \quad +$$
$$6 - 2 = 4$$
$$- \quad + \quad +$$
$$2 - 1 = 1$$
$$= \quad = \quad =$$
$$22 - 6 = 16$$

6)
$$36 - 8 + 2 = 30$$
$$+ \quad - \quad + \quad +$$
$$10 + 3 - 6 = 7$$
$$- \quad + \quad - \quad +$$
$$7 - 4 + 5 = 8$$
$$= \quad = \quad = \quad =$$
$$39 + 9 - 3 = 45$$

7)
$$50 - 13 + 5 + 9 = 51$$
$$+ \quad + \quad + \quad + \quad +$$
$$14 + 6 - 1 - 5 = 14$$
$$= \quad = \quad = \quad = \quad =$$
$$64 - 19 + 6 + 14 = 65$$

Day 99:

1)
$$50 \div 5 = 10$$
$$- \quad \times \quad \times$$
$$30 \div 6 = 5$$
$$= \quad = \quad =$$
$$20 + 30 = 50$$

2)
$$3 \times 10 = 30$$
$$+ \quad - \quad \div$$
$$10 - 7 = 3$$
$$= \quad = \quad =$$
$$13 - 3 = 10$$

3)
$$15 \div 5 = 3$$
$$+ \quad + \quad \times$$
$$30 - 10 = 20$$
$$= \quad = \quad =$$
$$45 + 15 = 60$$

4)
$$80 - 25 = 55$$
$$\div \quad \div \quad -$$
$$2 \times 5 = 10$$
$$= \quad = \quad =$$
$$40 + 5 = 45$$

5)
$$7 - 4 = 3$$
$$+ \quad \div \quad \times$$
$$8 + 2 = 10$$
$$= \quad = \quad =$$
$$15 \times 2 = 30$$

6)
$$40 \div 8 = 5$$
$$\div \quad - \quad +$$
$$10 \div 2 = 5$$
$$= \quad = \quad =$$
$$4 + 6 = 10$$

7)
$$10 \times 6 = 60$$
$$+ \quad \times \quad \div$$
$$12 \div 2 = 6$$
$$= \quad = \quad =$$
$$22 - 12 = 10$$

8)
$$2 \times 2 = 4$$
$$\times \quad + \quad \times$$
$$11 - 8 = 3$$
$$= \quad = \quad =$$
$$22 - 10 = 12$$

9)
$$13 + 5 = 18$$
$$\times \quad - \quad +$$
$$2 \times 4 = 8$$
$$= \quad = \quad =$$
$$26 \div 1 = 26$$

10)
$$70 - 15 - 35 = 20$$
$$\div \quad \div \quad - \quad +$$
$$7 + 3 + 10 = 20$$
$$= \quad = \quad = \quad =$$
$$10 + 5 + 25 = 40$$

11)
$$4 \times 8 = 32$$
$$+ \quad - \quad +$$
$$6 - 4 = 2$$
$$+ \quad - \quad +$$
$$2 \times 1 = 2$$
$$= \quad = \quad =$$
$$12 \times 3 = 36$$

12)
$$16 + 4 = 20$$
$$+ \quad + \quad -$$
$$32 \div 8 = 4$$
$$+ \quad - \quad +$$
$$12 - 6 = 6$$
$$= \quad = \quad =$$
$$60 \div 6 = 10$$

Day 100: Answers will vary.

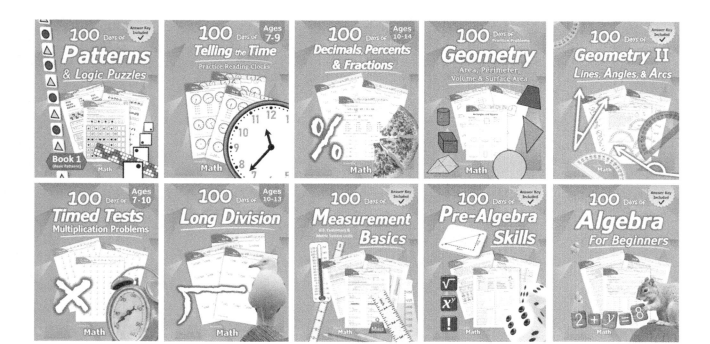

ISBN: 978-1-63578-407-7

Current contact information can be found at:
www.HumbleMath.com   www.LibroStudioLLC.com

Disclaimers:

50599739R00063